THE REFERENCE SHELF

Volume XVIII

No.
3. Representative American Speeches: 1944-1945. A. C. Baird. $1.25.
5. Anatomy of Racial Intolerance. G. B. de Huszar. $1.25.

No.
6. Palestine: Jewish Homeland? J. E. Johnsen. $1.25.

Volume XVII

No.
4. Representative American Speeches: 1943-1944. A. C. Baird. $1.25.

No.
5. Lowering the Voting Age. J. E. Johnsen. $1.25.

Volume XVI

No.
1. Representative American Speeches: 1941-1942. A. C. Baird. $1.25.
2. Plans for a Postwar World. J. E. Johnsen. $1.25.

No.
6. Representative American Speeches: 1942-1943. A. C. Baird. $1.25.
7. Reconstituting the League of Nations. J. E. Johnsen. $1.25.

Volume XV

No.
1. Representative American Speeches: 1940-1941. A. C. Baird. $1.25.
2. Universal Military Service. R. E. Summers and H. B. Summers. $1.25.
3. Federal Regulation of Labor Unions. J. V. Garland. $1.25.

No.
6. Wages and Prices. R. E. Summers. $1.25.
7. The Closed Shop. J. E. Johnsen. $1.25.
9. Permanent Price Control Policy. J. E. Johnsen. $1.25.
10. A Federal Sales Tax. E. R. Nichols. $1.25.

Volume XIV

No.
1. Representative American Speeches: 1939-1940. A. C. Baird. $1.50.
2. Interstate Trade Barriers. J. E. Johnsen. $1.25.
6. Compulsory Military Training. J. E. Johnsen. $1.25.

No.
8. International Federation of Democracies. J. E. Johnsen. $1.25.
9. Debate Index. Supplement. J. E. Johnsen. 75c.

Volume XIII

No.
4. Europe: Versailles to Warsaw. R. S. Kain. $1.25.
5. Public Housing in America. M. B. Schnapper. $1.25.
6. United States Foreign Policy (Supplement) J. E. Johnsen. 75c.

No.
9. The National Labor Relations Act. Should It Be Amended? J. E. Johnsen. $1.25.
10. Trade Unions and the Anti-Trust Laws. J. E. Johnsen. $1.25.

THE REFERENCE SHELF

Vol. 23   No. 2

REPRESENTATIVE AMERICAN SPEECHES: 1950-1951

Edited, and with Introductions,
by
A. CRAIG BAIRD
Department of Speech, State University of Iowa

THE H. W. WILSON COMPANY
NEW YORK   1951

PREFATORY NOTE

REPRESENTATIVE AMERICAN SPEECHES: 1950-51 is the fourteenth volume in this annual series. Each volume contains some twenty or more "representative" speeches, delivered by Americans or by others temporarily here (e.g. Charles H. Malik). The fourteen volumes include more than 300 addresses by some 230 speech makers.

The speeches are grouped according to context, such as United Nations, Korean War, Hydrogen Bomb, National Mobilization, Education, and Religion. An alternate classification, based upon speech occasions, may also be followed by students interested in speeches of introduction, those of Congress, court room, pulpit, luncheon or dinners, political campaigns, business or other professional gatherings.

This editor, as he has done in previous volumes, disavows the assumption that these are the "best" speeches of the year, or that the 300 addresses of these combined volumes are the "best" of recent times. They are, he hopes, "representative" of the kind and quality of American public addresses given during a given period. Each speech, we hope, touches upon an idea or issue of interest to millions of listeners. Some of these speeches, we are confident, have made an impress on recent American history.

The Introduction to each of the fourteen volumes deals with some phase of the problems of speech standards. Together these partial treatments both explain the point of view of this editor in this annual publication and give clues to his own philosophy of speech preparation and delivery.

The brief introduction accompanying each speech suggests (all too briefly, in some cases) the background and immediate occasion. Factors of thought, forms of support, structure, language, the speaker's audience adjustment, delivery, and immediate results of the presentation are also touched upon—to suggest that the student explore further these elements of the given discourse. "The assumption of this critic is that speech is for social adaptation; that it springs from immediate situations; and that the attitudes and trends of American life [of 1950-51] are partly revealed through this volume."

The biographical notes in the Appendix invite extended review of each speaker. Knowledge of the orator's education, professional and other experiences, especially his speaking record, will obviously increase the reader's ability to evaluate the sample under examination.

The Table of Contents of each edition and the Cumulated Author Index at the end of this volume are further aids in a review of the speakers and issues of the years since 1937. The later speaking career of Franklin D. Roosevelt, for example, can be studied by tracing his utterances in the successive volumes.

This volume, like its predecessors, is a reference source for the study of contemporary problems; a partial record of recent months; and a collection of examples that may help the learner in his own progress in speech composition and delivery. Each volume, in addition to its service as a library reference, is especially recommended to students of extempore speaking and communication, debate, social science, history, and general public speaking and to teachers of these subjects.

This editor is heavily indebted to various speakers for permission to reproduce their speeches and for their cooperation in providing authentic texts. I am also grateful to publishers and organizations that have permitted the reprinting of the speeches. Specific acknowledgement is made in the footnote accompanying each address.

A. CRAIG BAIRD

April 8, 1951

CONTENTS

INTRODUCTION

HOW SHALL WE JUDGE THE DELIVERY OF A SPEECH?

How shall we judge the delivery of a speech? Students of rhetoric and speech-making have long agreed that the principal components of a speech include (1) thought or ideas (2) structure or organization (3) language or style and (4) delivery. In previous introductions to these annual collections I have discussed at some length the method and criticism of thought and language.[1]

I propose here to summarize briefly the principles of delivery and the standards by which one may judge the effectiveness of delivery in a given speech. These principles and standards, familiar to all teachers of speech, are here offered as a design for speech criticism as well as a suggestive basis by which the student may improve his own delivery.[2]

Delivery concerns itself specifically with four aspects. First is the voice itself. Good voice calls for acceptable pitch, rate, intensity, quality, and for efficient articulation and pronunciation. Second is the accompanying bodily activity, including gesture, posture, and movement. Third is the speaker's personality. The physical, emotional, intellectual, and other elements of personality contribute importantly to the speaking results. Fourth is the manuscript reading, memoriter, or extempore mode of communicating the speech to the listeners.

In comment on these four components of delivery we make no attempt to assign relative weight on a speech scale. We cannot categorically rate intensity as more significant than vocal rate. All depends upon the man, the time, place, and audience, and upon the total effect. Speaking is not a science but an art. We are hardly justified in applying a hard and fast formula for measuring effectiveness. One speaker may succeed because of his

[1] *Representative American Speeches: 1948-49*, p7-13; *Representative American Speeches: 1949-50*, p7-14.

[2] For detailed guidance in speech improvement, the learner is referred to any representative speech text.

voice quality; another, without organ-like resonance, may excel through his deep sincerity and vocal energy. The standards outlined below are suggestive only. These basic criteria of excellence in delivery admit of wide variation in the application.

1. *The superior speaker has desirable vocal pitch.* His natural pitch level on the musical scale and his pitch changes are fully acceptable to auditors. His voice is neither too high nor too low. He has vocal flexibility, free from continually rising inflections, singsong, and other disturbing pitch patterns. His intonations and vocal shifts register emotional activity consonant with the meaning. His vocal control thus aids his rhetorical rapport with his audience.

2. *The superior speaker has effective vocal intensity or loudness.* He is neither unduly soft-spoken nor noisy. He adjusts his voice to the size of the room (to the open-air situation, or to the microphone), to the occasion, and to the purposes of his message. He regulates his breathing to supply air sufficient to sustain vocalization. His volume is produced without undue strain on his vocal mechanism or throat. Vocally he is relaxed, free from breathiness, loudness, monotony. His clear articulation also helps the audience to easy listening. His degree of loudness conveys effectively the emotional and intellectual content of his ideas.

3. *The superior speaker controls his vocal rate.* Time, duration, or rate, he relates to his pitch and intensity. He is neither so fast as to baffle comprehension nor so slow as to bore. He avoids a wild gallop or a dull jog. He is without excess nonfluencies either silent (awkward pauses) or vocal ("and-uh's"). He does not speak with artificial prolongation of vowels and consonants. His rate may be as slow as a hundred words per minute—normal for him in the speaking situation—or he may normally deliver a hundred and seventy-five words per minute. He knows his audience, talks directly to individuals. He is vocally animated, pleasant and persuasive. These factors determine his variability rate. In short he is effective in his control of vocal rate.

4. *The superior speaker should have excellent voice quality.* His tones convey vocal harmony, richness of resonance, a satis-

factory blending of overtones in the resonators. His mouth, teeth, tongue, hard and soft palate are properly adjusted to provide satisfactory resonance. He has no marked nasality, harshness, hoarseness, gutteral heaviness, shrillness, thinness, stridency, metallic or muffled quality. His utterance is balanced between tension and relaxation and is pleasing to the ear.

5. *The superior speaker projects to his audience.* He establishes and maintains circular response. He and the group become mutually stimulating. Complete audience rapport results. He is physically and mentally alert, active rather than passive. He utilizes his voice, eye contact, general bodily activity to attract and hold attention. He dominates but does so unobtrusively. Always he has a lively sense of communication.

6. *The superior speaker uses the conversational mode.* Even though the occasion gives birth to high oratory, the speaker retains the intimacy, directness, and naturalness of conversation. He loses nothing of public vehemence and decisiveness, but always he is communicating as one conferee to another. The best of conversational idiom is evident in his tones. He has complete reaction to the words he is voicing. His rate, intensity, vocal changes are all related to the full expression of his thought.

7. *The superior speaker is efficient in articulation and pronunciation.* The supreme speaker is normal, unaffected, in his method of articulating vowels and consonants. His vowels are pure, unmistakable; his consonants are fully yet not heavily sounded. He makes no fetish of perfection in his shaping of sounds. His voiced b, d, and g, and his voiceless p, t, k, and h are distinct but not artifically sounded. He is no purist. But he is not lip lazy nor given to hesitations and similar distractions. His main concern is with the communication of his ideas.

His pronunciation is socially acceptable. He has a minimum of pronunciation errors of substitution (*fer* for *for*), addition (*athelete* for *athlete*), omission (*w'y* for *why*), inversion (*calvery* for *cavalry*), and misplaced accents (*a'dult* for *adult'*). He is not given to pseudo-cultured speech, obvious affectation. His regional speech has also "General American" elements. Most of the educated people of his region or of the nation at large who hear him find little to disturb their ears.

BODILY ACTIVITY

The superior speaker recognizes that in communication, visible behavior is almost as decisive as tones. Because most people are primarily visual minded, posture, gesture, and movement become key agents of oral expression.

8. *The superior speaker has impressive physical bearing.* His posture, although it may not be of commanding physical proportions, is nevertheless dominating. It conveys meaning to the observer-auditor. The speaker is erect, dignified without being military. His posture is natural and easy, his body relaxed, yet enlisting respect and attention. He does not slouch, stoop, tip, sway, or push his hands aimlessly about. He conveys an impression of self-control, purpose, ease, freedom, and friendliness. He begets confidence in his leadership.

9. *The superior speaker communicates effectively by his bodily activity on the platform.* His movements are not excessive, calculated, mechanical. Rather he moves easily, spontaneously, in company with the changes in his ideas. He is not circumscribed by the rostrum, the microphone, or by his manuscript. He has no barrier to separate him from his audience. Impelled by his ideas, he escapes from passivity or inertia. His movements are determined by his temperament and cultural habits, by the character, size, and physical surroundings of the audience, and by the occasion itself.

10. *The superior speaker uses effective gestures.* The movements of his hands, arms, shoulders, head, and eyes harmonize with the gross bodily changes. His gestures are forcible, emphatic, descriptive, or impressive. They are not random, erratic, protracted without purpose, meaningless. He is no windmill. He is free from physical mannerisms and emotional instability. The subject possesses him and his bodily activity contributes to the realization of his speech purposes.

THE SPEAKER'S PERSONALITY

Personality—the total physical, mental and emotional resources and activities of the individual—strongly affects delivery.

11. *The superior speaker's public character and reputation reenforces his oral presentation.* His prestige, the product of his

previous professional public speaking career, is a part of his equipment as he approaches each new speaking situation. This factor adds to his ethical or personal proofs and blends with his voice, movements, and gestures to enhance his persuasive delivery.

12. *The superior speaker has emotional control and balance.* Although his performance is accompanied by vigorous audience projection and quickened energy, he nevertheless wisely directs his emotional behavior and closely integrates it with his voice, bodily activity and ideas. His presentation reflects self-confidence and courage. He is not pompous, egotistic, or offensively assertive. His emotional poise invites confidence in him and faith in his ideas.

13. *The superior speaker appeals by his intellectual and moral behavior.* He has the power to recall vividly a wide variety of experiences and ability to demonstrate the details with mental ease and clarity. Toward his problem he is open minded and intellectually honest. He impresses by his sincerity and conviction. His social outlook is also well developed. He is cooperative and has confidence in the judgments of society. His interest in the problems of others is genuine. He has a passion for truth and patience in expounding it. His motives are the highest. He is "a good man speaking well."

ORAL MANUSCRIPT READING, MEMORITER, AND EXTEMPORE MODES OF DELIVERY

Superior speakers are by no means uniform in their methods of presenting their prepared speeches. Some read the manuscript; others memorize the script; still others prefer the extempore method. The same speaker may vary his method according to the occasion and audience. Albert J. Beveridge, for example, in his earlier public career, often memorized and delivered verbatim his addresses. In his later years in the Senate and on the stump he was effective in extempore delivery.

14. *The superior speaker who reads his address does so creatively and effectively.* He has a lively sense of communication. Audiences are little conscious of his reading, so little is he tied to his pages, so fully has he mentally appropriated the sense of his message.

15. *The superior speaker who memorizes retains all the elements of conversational delivery.* Like the one who reads, he concentrates on meanings and upon the audience. His delivery reflects a deep appreciation of the full content of what he has previously composed.

16. *The superior speaker is effective in extemporization.* All experienced and able public speakers are at home with audiences and language. The minds of these orators work freely, their vocabulary and vocal fluency are more than adequate. Whether or not these extempore speakers rely upon an outline, they have assimilated their prepared ideas. These extemporizers move confidently through their speeches, with constant improvisations of ideas and illustrations, and with all the vocal skill that gives high distinction to their delivery.

The rise of television has greatly increased the importance of effective delivery and extempore speaking.

Delivery and Total Effectiveness

17. *The superior speaker rates high in total speaking effectiveness.* Our estimate of "superior" speaking is determined not by focusing upon each external aspect of delivery, such as pitch or rate, but rather by taking account of the totality of the delivery elements. Furthermore our judgment of the superior public speaker is based not upon concentration upon delivery, ideas, language, and organization as separate concepts, but upon the combination of these rhetorical skills. We isolate them for description. But the great speaker, as we have often remarked, utilizes these functions as a single process. Seldom does any one orator excel in all the categories. In the total interplay of these elements, however, the speakers we single out as superior rank high.[3]

[3] *See Representative American Speeches: 1946-1947,* "What Constitutes an Effective Speech?" p7-12.

UNITED NATIONS AND KOREA

THE BIG LIE [1] ·

WARREN R. AUSTIN [2]

Ambassador Warren R. Austin, United States Representative to the United Nations, gave this speech before the Security Council on August 22, 1950. Since Tuesday, August 1, the Council had been intermittently in session, with Mr. Jacob Malik, of Russia, as President.

During that time not one bit of constructive business had been accomplished. The simple fact was that Russia, with its veto power, could successfully block any anti-Soviet measure proposed by the United Nations sponsors. One August session succeeded another, each filled with vituperation and propagandistic recrimination. The continued refrain was, "America was the aggressor in starting the South Korean war." The vocal barrage was focussed against this country with comparatively light attack upon our Allies.

The program of Wednesday, August 22, for example, opened with Malik's long harangue, some ten thousand words and occupying several hours, in which the Russian detailed the American aggression in Korea and repeated again the arguments he had often recited. Following further parliamentary exchange, Sir Gladwyn Jebb, of Britain, spoke at length in measured rebuttal filled with logic and delivered with sarcasm. Mr. Austin then followed.

Some of the proceedings of this Council under the presidency of the Soviet Union representative must certainly have filled with misgivings the hearts of people all over the world who believe in the United Nations and look to it as their best hope for preventing another world war.

With the eyes of the world upon us, the actions of the Soviet Union representative in subverting the presidency of the Security Council have obstructed even the commonplace and regular procedures historically recognized as necessary for substantive decisions. I will not recount those actions. I will only observe that there can now be no doubt who it is amongst us that

[1] Text furnished through the courtesy of the United States Mission to the United Nations.

[2] For biographical note, see Appendix.

seeks every opportunity to frustrate the hopes of peace-loving people. The statement made to us by the Soviet Union representative at our last meeting has dispelled all doubt.

There are a few aspects of the recent statements to this Council by the representative of the Soviet Union to which I will refer. Before doing so, I refer to the repeated efforts of the Soviet Union representative implying that everyone who fails to agree with him is, *ipso facto*, a satellite of the United States. I can understand how difficult it must be for the distinguished Soviet Union representative to comprehend that not all big nations browbeat all smaller nations whenever and wherever the opportunity arises. It is a natural conclusion to be drawn from a knowledge of Soviet foreign policy.

Apparently, the Soviet Union representative can conceive of relationships between nations only in terms of power, in terms of the stronger dominating the weaker. Therefore, whenever he sees other countries support the same principle the United States supports, he concludes my government has enmeshed them in some brutish stratagem. This is a philosophy worthy of some witch-doctor who has created so many soulless zombies in his own graveyard that he ends up believing the earth is peopled entirely by such creatures.

The Soviet Union representative could not be more mistaken. The earth is peopled by men and women who believe in individual liberty and national independence. If the Soviet Union representative would brush the scales of an antique doctrine from his eyes, he could see for himself the true aspirations of peoples of every race and creed; he could understand that men and nations will act together when the liberties they cherish jointly were at stake; he could understand that, inside and outside the United Nations, on every continent men will vote together, will act together, and will make common sacrifice because they firmly adhere to the great principles on which peace and freedom must rest.

If the Soviet Union representative understood these things, we might then have an end to his futile efforts to make black white, and white black. We might be spared more of the fantastic version of events with which the Soviet Union representative has sought to catch the unwary and confuse the uninformed.

The most persistent distortion has been the Soviet Union representative's insistence that a peaceful settlement of the Korean issue would be advanced if the representatives of the North Korean aggressors were to be seated at this Council table. This, in fact, appears to be the major Soviet Union proposal for a "peaceful settlement." It is like arguing that an assassin should be allowed to justify his act while still plunging his knife into the body of his victim. Such a "peaceful" proposal can lead only to the peace of the graveyard.

We are told we should place the invader, who has an unbroken record of defiance of the United Nations, before us on an equal footing with the Republic of Korea which was established with the help of the United Nations and which the General Assembly has found to be the only lawful government in Korea. We are told to invite the malefactor to this table while he continues to defy our authority and denounce our decisions.

The course of action proposed by the Soviet Union representative would place a premium on aggression. Whether or not that is the Soviet Union purpose that would be its effect. The North Koreans are presented to us by the Soviet Union representative as a party to a dispute. This, he tells us, is "The fact." This is not a dispute. Even the Soviet Union representative must be aware that fifty-three members of the United Nations are in agreement that North Korea is an aggressor—and that this is a breach of the peace. Therefore, we can have no thought of hearing the aggressor so long as he continues his defiance.

The Soviet Union representative has read to this Council copies of the falsehoods being spread all over the world by misguided minorities who support Communist imperialism. Mr. President, it is not necessary to answer each falsehood, one by one. All one needs is to expose the tricks of propaganda which are being used here.

Contempt for the intelligence of men and women lies behind every propaganda device which is not based on truth. A number of such devices are clearly discernible in the recent statements made to this Council by the Soviet Union representative. Today, I deal with only three of them: the "false label" trick, the trick of "concealing guilt by accusation," and finally, the trick now generally known as the techniques of the "Big Lie."

Let us consider first the "false label" trick. Here falsehood is presented as fact. Accordingly, the propagandist keeps saying, "This is an irrefutable fact," or begins the falsehood with the phrase, "as is well known." Of course nothing of the sort is well known, or the Soviet Union representative would not waste the time by repeating distortions of the record and trying to sell them as facts.

There is a simple way to expose the "false label" trick. When the housewife cans her fruits and vegetables in the fall, she puts a label on each jar before storing it away. If she puts the label "peaches" on a jar containing applesauce the label does not magically change the contents. One can quickly test the label by opening the jar and sampling the real thing inside.

Let us examine the jar placed before the Security Council by the representative of the Soviet Union. He said that no United Nations tags nor flags sent by Mr. Lie to General Mac-Arthur could hide the stark fact of United States aggression. He said that today. The Soviet Union representative told the Council, in a speech which he made before this one:

"After provoking this conflict and seeing that the political regime of Syngman Rhee was collapsing, the United States resorted to open intervention." Now, here comes the label trick: "Such are the irrefutable facts, and the United States representative is not in a position to deny them."

Sir, I am in a position to open that falsely labeled jar and let the world see what is inside—applesauce. I welcome the opportunity, in answer, to give wider circulation to the report of the United Nations Commission on Korea, contained in its cablegram of 26 June 1950.

The report said in part: "For the past two years the North Korean regime has by violently abusive propaganda, by threatening gestures along the 38th parallel and by encouraging and supporting subversive activities in the territory of the Republic of Korea, pursued tactics designed to weaken and destroy the Government of the Republic of Korea established under the auspices of the United Nations Temporary Commission on Korea and recognized by the General Assembly."

Do you know of any more independent, unbiased witness?

The message from these official observers of the United Nations goes on to describe the elections of 30 May 1950, which were "successfully conducted in an atmosphere of law and order," with all parties except the underground Communist Party participating. The Commission reports: "There have been distinct signs of improvement in recent months in both economic and political stability of the country."

The 30 May 1950 elections produced a new National Assembly "with some hundred and thirty Independents out of a total of two hundred ten members." That is more than half. The party which received a majority of 1948 lost its majority to other parties.

It is true that in those states controlled by the Soviet Union Government, the political party which directs the police force never loses the election. Perhaps that is the difficulty. Perhaps it is the inability of the Soviet Union representative to conceive of an election going against the party which it assumes must control the police. The President charged in the Security Council today that American *gauleiters* and United States monopolists imposed the Government on South Korea. But, Mr. President, in the free world any party may win an election. Perhaps the Soviet Union representative is also confused by the fact that the people of Korea—the people of Korea—were offered a choice of political parties for which they might vote. But, Mr. President, in the free world that does happen.

The secret ballot, cast without fear or intimidation, and counted fairly, gives every man a voice in his own destiny. Could it be that this is the thought the Soviet Union representative has in mind when he refers, as he so often does, to the "ruling circles" of the United States? There are ruling circles in the United States, different from those to which the President refers. There is a total, according to the last census, of over 150 million "ruling circles." I fear, however, that in the Soviet Union there is but one "ruling circle." If the day should arrive that the people of the Soviet Union are free to vote for more than one party, we might be able to refer to the "ruling circles" of the Soviet Union. If that day should arrive, we might be able to say that the Soviet Union had made a striking advance toward the democracy already achieved within the Republic of Korea.

The facts, far from showing the collapse of the political regime in the Republic of Korea, demonstrate the opposite. In spite of the tactics of the Communists to weaken and destroy the Republic from within, the new Republic, by democratic methods, strengthened itself in the election of 30 May 1950. The obvious conclusion is that when the North Korean regime found it could not take the Republic from within, it launched its aggression to take it by force of arms from without. The United Nations acted with dispatch and unity. The United States supported that United Nations action. The old "label trick" did not work. Not even the label devised here today by the President can stick. He labels it "a colossal international bluff." Events daily expose this type of trick.

Another declaration boldly labeled as a "fact" is the Soviet Union claim here that the North Koreans have only the armaments sold to them by the Soviet Union Government when the Red Army withdrew. This so-called "fact" should be tested against such evidence as the plainly labeled Soviet shell marked "1950" which United Nations forces have uncovered. This shell did not explode on the battlefield. It explodes in the Security Council. I think we might properly call it a misguided missile. Of course, I recognize that this may be just another case of false Soviet labeling.

Now let us consider the trick of concealing guilt through accusation. The classic example of this trick, of course, is that of the thief who, in running away from the policemen, cries "stop thief" at the honest men ahead of him in order to confuse the pursuers. This is the type of trick that has been employed in an effort to prove that the North Korean invaders merely have been defending themselves from an attack by the Republic of Korea.

In using this technique, the Soviet Union representative forgets that the record of every aggressor in recent times is fresh in people's minds. Let us cite only two examples from the record of the master aggressor.

Hitler, on 1 September 1939, having concluded his Pact of Friendship with the Soviet Union and a secret protocol agreeing to the division of Poland with the Soviet Union, declared that "the Polish State has rejected a peaceful solution of the problem of neighbourly relations with Germany," and that "force must be met by force." "The battle," declared Hitler, "will be fought in defense of German territory and honor."

The Nazi dictator employed the same old thief calling "stop thief" technique when he launched his dastardly attack on the Soviet Union in 1941. On 22 June 1941, in justifying the Nazi march against the Soviet Union, Hitler said: "During the night of 17 June to 18 June, Russian patrols again penetrated into the Reich's territory and could only be driven back by prolonged firing. This has brought us to the hour when it is necessary for us to take steps against this plot devised by the Jewish Anglo-Saxon warmongers and equally the Jewish rulers of the Bolshevist center in Moscow."

The Hitler deception did not succeed. Aggression was crushed, and the weapons we produced as part of our contribution were toasted by Generalissimo Stalin at Teheran as necessary to the victory of the Soviet Union against the Hitlerite aggressors.

This same trick of covering one's own guilt by accusing others of the crime is employed in the recurring statement that the fight in Korea is nothing but an extension of American imperialism. For example, the Soviet Union representative told us the other day that "United States ruling circles are now attempting to pervert the whole of the United Nations into a weapon for the defense of American capital investments." We have heard him repeat that charge in other language today. Indeed, he says that we have draped the flag of the United Nations over the United States in order to hide the aggression by the United States.

The representative of China on Thursday last expounded the nature of Soviet imperialism in Asia as it is today. It is the revival and extension of ancient Czarist imperialism which has developed human exploitation to the high degree represented in the systematic looting of Manchuria and the absorption of Outer Mongolia.

What are the facts concerning Korea? Of course, we have never been permitted to obtain knowledge of the economic relationship between the North Korean "zombie" regime and the Soviet Union. Therefore, we are left to ask, what are the diabolical American investments which they say the "ruling circles" of the United States are protecting? Who are the monopolists about which Mr. Malik makes the accusation today—an accusation made for a purpose.

It is true that Americans for decades have been making "investments" in Korea. These investments are of a very special kind. They are investments in churches, schools, hospitals and clinics. They are investments in the uplifting of the Korean people, ministering to the hungry, the sick and the heavy laden. Missionaries, teachers, doctors, and nurses are the "monopolists" and "ruling circles" you are talking about, sir.

Aside from these investments of mercy, let us see what the facts are concerning those "investments" to which you referred today by name, Mr. President.

Gilbert Associates, which the President mentioned, is in Korea to conduct an electric power survey designed to increase the amount of electric power available to the people of Korea. It is not a construction concern. Its primary purpose is to help South Korea replace the electric power which formerly came from North Korea but which was cut off arbitrarily by the Soviet Union occupation forces. In 1948 at the time of the elections, the Soviet Union occupation forces in North Korea sought to terrorize the people in the South by putting obstructions in the way of sale of electric power to the South. The refusal to sell power to the Republic, initiated by the Soviet authorities has been continued by the Northern "zombie" regime. Gilbert Associates performed a service for which it received a fee. That is as sinister as that operation has ever been.

Let us look at the Tungsten Associates to which the representative of the Soviet Union referred. It is owned by the Republic of Korea. It sells tungsten to all buyers including buyers from countries other than the United States. That is the truth in that case.

The Korean Oil Storage Company is a warehouse and distribution operation. It is not a "monopoly." Competitive opportunities are unrestricted. The learned "ruling circle" of the Soviet Union can use this as one of its biggest lies.

At Kimpo Airfield a concern named Bourne Associates has been employed to reconstruct the field for the benefit of the Koreans. It owned no part of the field. At the time of the invasion, it was temporarily operating the tower of the field and performing other services at the request of the Korean authorities.

The criterion of any investment is whether or not it produces profits, is it not? Can the representative of the Soviet Union prove that any of the operations he mentioned has ever resulted in dollar remittances out of Korea? He can not. The United States has put millions of dollars into Korea for the assistance of the people of Korea. That, Mr. President, is the fact.

Here is one final example of the technique of accusing the innocent in order to conceal guilt.

One fourth of a recent speech by the representative of the Soviet Union was devoted to efforts to discredit the objective testimony of the United Nations Commission on Korea. He asserted that the "composition of the Commission is in no way a guarantee of its objectivity" and referred to "fabricated reports of the Commission dictated by MacArthur." This is an insult to the seven nations represented on this Commission, namely, Australia, China, El Salvador, France, India, the Philippines and Turkey, and to the majority of the General Assembly which established and is supporting that Commission, and which still supports that Commission.

The representative of the Soviet Union rejects the unanimous judgment of these seven men from these seven countries, based on on-the-spot observations, that North Koreans launched an unprovoked attack. If you do not accept the word of the United Nations Commission, whose word can you take? The Soviet Union wants us to take their word on who started it—but they claim they were not even there.

I come now to the propaganda trick with which the world has had the saddest experience within the past fifteen years. It is commonly known as the technique of the "Big Lie."

Hitler spread the theory that if a propagandist will not tire of repeating an assertion, no matter how preposterous, he can make it stick in many minds. That is easier to do if no one is allowed to contradict the propagandist and confront him with facts. But here in the United Nations we can confront him with facts.

In his speech at the last meeting of this Council the representative of the Soviet Union referred several times to "the aggression of which the United States is guilty against the Korean people." This statement has been repeated over and over through every Soviet-inspired channel on earth. We have had it telegraphed to us by others, and we have heard it again today. It is a lie. It is a "Big Lie."

Today Mr. Malik asked: What was Mr. Austin proposing? And he answered his own question. First, he said, the representative of the United States was proposing a continuation of the war and increasing the scope of aggression; and second, a return to the General Assembly resolutions on Korea. The representative of the United States, he said, would like to pass those resolutions which would mean a return to the Syngman Rhee regime. This also meant that not only South Korea but the whole of Korea was to become an American colony, under American monopolists and American *gauleiters.*

This is a beautiful example of the "Big Lie."

Only in the weird world of Soviet propaganda is there any doubt concerning the origin of the aggression in Korea. The aggressor is the regime established in Pyonpyang when the Soviet Union was in military occupation of North Korea. The aggressor is the North Korean regime which was established in direct defiance of the United Nations and which has continued to defy both the Security Council and the General Assembly.

United States forces did not start the aggression in Korea. United States forces came to Korea only in support of Security Council action to repel North Korean aggression. To call the action of those governments who are seeking to support the

resolutions of the Security Council an act of aggression, is a
falsehood so grotesque that even the technique of the Big Lie
cannot disguise it.

These, Mr. President, are the facts.

The Security Council acted on Sunday 25 June, calling for
immediate cessation of hostilities and withdrawal of the North
Korean forces forthwith. That same resolution, adopted by nine
votes to none, called upon "all members to render every assistance to the United Nations in the execution of this resolution
and to refrain from giving assistance to the North Korean
authorities." Let us not forget that last phrase in the resolution,
"to refrain from giving assistance to the North Korean authorities."

If the North Korean authorities had obeyed that order within
the next twenty-four hours, there would have been no need for
the Security Council resolution of 27 June, nor would police
action in support of the United Nations have been required. The
Security Council's order is still being defied by the North Korean
regime and by those who support it. No tricks of repetition can
cover up that big truth.

This attempt to turn black into white by saying black is white
can be exposed by two simple questions.

Did the Soviet Union bring to the Security Council on 25
June a complaint that the United States had made an armed
attack on North Korea?

Did the Soviet Union bring to the Security Council a complaint that the Republic of Korea had invaded North Korea?

No. The ruling circle at Moscow had ample time in which
to do that. Their failure is consistent only with the fact that
the aggressor was the North Koreans.

We have heard many declarations from the representative of
the Soviet Union to the effect that the Soviet Union desires a
peaceful settlement in Korea. No doubt we will hear more such
declarations. Unfortunately, our experience to date causes us
to treat this statement with reserve until we find evidence that
the Soviet Union will act for peace as well as talk for peace.

My country is sacrificing the lives of many of its young men
in order to bring real peace to Korea. Other members of the

United Nations are making or are preparing to make similar sacrifices. We, therefore, have urgent reason for taking action, compatible with United Nations objectives, to attain peace in Korea.

The representative of the Soviet Union spoke to us on Thursday of the influence of his government and how able it is to exert influence in international affairs. Why not let us see that influence employed in the cause of peace. We know that if the Soviet Union Government wanted the fighting stopped in Korea, it could be stopped today. Therefore, I hope the Soviet Union representative will understand if there is disgust at his apparent disposition to regard peace only as an item of conversation.

My government is working for peace, sacrificing for peace. So are fifty-two other members of the United Nations. Our words are backed up by deeds.

Mr. President, I think I need say no more today concerning the propaganda tricks employed by the representative of the Soviet Union.

The real task before us is to dispose of propaganda tricks, to stop dodging the real issues of the Korean conflict, and to carry forward with the central issue of restoring peace and security to the area. This requires the regular order.

UNITED NATIONS AND
SOVIET AGGRESSION [3]

DEAN ACHESON [4]

Dean Acheson, Secretary of State, gave this address before the General Assembly of the United Nations, at Lake Success, New York, on September 20, 1950. The United Nations Security Council had convened at Flushing Meadows on the previous day for its 1950 session. Its first business was the rejection of the Indian and Soviet proposals for the admission of Communist China to the General Assembly. The Assembly then rejected the Soviet proposal for the admission of the Chinese People's Republic. Mr. Acheson on the next day was the first great power representative to present directly the real issues to be faced by the Assembly with respect to Formosa, China, Korea, and the Soviet Union.

His was a long speech, carefully prepared and organized, impressively read. Its significance, aside from the maturity of its expression and its political philosophy, lay in its proposal that the General Assembly, in case the Security Council was unable to act, should immediately convene to insure positive action on critical decisions.

The second division of his address, really a separate speech, was a proposal for a "recovery force" to rebuild a peaceful world. This "second speech" was generally regarded as an appeal to Asiatic countries. The address was obviously designed to influence world opinion. Its sentiments were no doubt heartening to the small nations as well as to more important allies.

At his best on such formal occasions in the presence of the representatives of sixty nations, Mr. Acheson was suave, cultured, vocally emphatic, and logical. His bearing and language, however, reflected the diplomatic reserve of the State Department.[5]

Mr. President, fellow delegates, people of the United Nations: This meeting of the General Assembly is a meeting of decision. Before us lies opportunity for action which can save the hope of peace, security, well-being, and justice for generations to come. Before us also lies opportunity for drift, for irresolution, for effort feebly made. In this direction is disaster. The

---

[3] Text furnished by the Department of State.
[4] For biographical note, see Appendix.
[5] See also *Representative American Speeches: 1948-1949,* p15-26.

choice is ours. It will be made whether we act or whether we do not act.

The peoples of the world know this. They will eagerly follow every word spoken here. Our words will reach them mingled with the sound of the battle now raging in Korea. There, men are fighting and dying under the banner of the United Nations. Our charter, born out of the sacrifices of millions in war, is being consecrated anew to peace at the very moment of our meeting. The heroism of these men gives us this opportunity to meet and to act. Our task is to be worthy of them and of that opportunity.

We meet also with full knowledge of the great anxiety which clutches at the hearts of the people of this earth. Men and women everywhere are weighted down with fear—fear of war, fear that man may be begetting his own destruction.

But man is not a helpless creature who must await an inexorable fate. It lies within our power to take action which, God willing, can avert the catastrophe whose shadow hangs over us. That terrible responsibility rests upon every man and woman in this room. At the end of this meeting each of us must answer to his conscience on what we have done here.

How have we come to this condition of fear and jeopardy? The lifetime of many here has seen the rise and fall of empires, the growth of powerful nations, the stirrings of great continents with new-born hope, the conquest of space, and great inventions, both creative and destructive. We have lived in a century of alternating war and hope.

Now, the foundation of our hope is the United Nations. Five years ago we declared at San Francisco our determination "to save succeeding generations from the scourge of war," our faith in fundamental human rights, our belief in justice and social progress. During these years, some of us have worked hard to bring this about.

There is no longer any question: Will the United Nations survive? Will the United Nations suffer the fate of the League of Nations? This question has been answered. If by nothing else, it has been answered by United Nations action against aggression in Korea. Blood is thicker than ink.

But a pall of fear has been cast over our hopes and our achievements. What is the reason for this fear? Why is it that we have been unable to achieve peace and security through the United Nations in these five years? Why has there not been the cooperation among the great powers which was to have buttressed the United Nations? Why have we not been able to reach an agreement on the control of atomic energy and the regulation of armaments? What has been the obstacle to a universal system of collective security?

We have been confronted with many and complex problems, but the main obstacle to peace is easy to identify, and there should be no mistake in anyone's mind about it. That obstacle has been created by the policies of the Soviet Government.

We should be very clear in our minds about this obstacle. It is not the rise of the Soviet Union as a strong national power, which creates difficulties. It is not the existence of different social and economic systems in the world. Nor is it, I firmly believe, any desire on the part of the Russian people for war. The root of our trouble is to be found in the new imperialism, directed by the leaders of the Soviet Union.

To be more explicit, the Soviet Government raises five barriers to peace.

First, Soviet efforts to bring about the collapse of the non-Soviet world, and thereby fulfill a prediction of Soviet theory, have made genuine negotiation very difficult. The Honorable Representative of Lebanon, Dr. Charles Malik, stated it precisely at our last assembly when he said: "There can be no greater disagreement than when one wants to eliminate your existence altogether."

Second, the shroud of secrecy which the Soviet leaders have wrapped around the people and the states they control is a great barrier to peace. This has nourished suspicion and misinformation, in both directions. It deprives governments of the moderating influence of contact between peoples. It stands in the way of the mutual knowledge and confidence essential to disarmament.

Third, the rate at which the Soviet Union has been building arms and armies, far beyond any requirement of defense, has gravely endangered peace throughout the world. While other countries were demobilizing and converting their industries to peaceful purposes after the war, the Soviet Union and the territories under its control pushed preparation for war. The Soviet Union has forced countries to rearm for their self-defense.

Fourth, the use by Soviet leaders of the international Communist movement for direct and indirect aggression has been a great source of trouble in the world. With words which play upon honest aspirations and grievances, the Soviet leaders have manipulated the people of other states as pawns of Russian imperialism.

Fifth, the Soviet use of violence to impose its will and its political system upon other people is a threat to the peace. There is nothing unusual in the fact that those who believe in some particular social order want to spread it throughout the world. But as one of my predecessors, Secretary Adams, said of the efforts of an earlier Russian ruler, Czar Alexander, to establish the Holy Alliance, the Emperor "finds a happy coincidence between the dictates of his conscience and the interests of his empire." The combination of this international ambition and the Soviet reliance on force and violence—though it be camouflaged as civil war—is a barrier to peaceful relations.

This conduct conflicts with the Charter of the United Nations. It conflicts with the "Essentials of Peace" Resolution passed at our last Assembly. It has created a great and terrible peril for the rest of the world.

Even this conduct has not made war inevitable—we, for our part, do not accept the idea that war is inevitable. But it has lengthened the shadow of war. This fact cannot be obscured by propaganda which baits the hooks with words of peace, and in doing so profanes the highest aspirations of mankind.

There is only one real way the world can maintain peace and security in the face of this conduct. That is by strengthening its system of collective security. Our best hope of peace lies in our ability to make absolutely plain to potential aggressors that aggression cannot succeed. The security of those nations who want peace and the security of the United Nations itself, demands the strength to prevent further acts of aggression.

One of the fundamental purposes of the United Nations, as expressed in Article 1 of the Charter, is that it shall ". . . take effective collective measures for the prevention and removal of threats to the peace, and for the suppression of acts of aggression or other breaches of peace. . . ."

The action of the United Nations to put down the aggression which began on June 25th against the Republic of Korea was exactly the effective collective measure required. It marked a turning point in history, for it showed the way to an enforceable rule of law among nations.

The world waits to see whether we can build on the start we have made. The United Nations must move forward energetically to develop a more adequate system of collective security. If it does not move forward it will move back.

Article 24 of the Charter gives the Security Council primary responsibility for the maintenance of peace. This is the way it should be. But if the Security Council is not able to act because of the obstructive tactics of a permanent member, the Charter does not leave the United Nations impotent. The obligation of all members to take action to maintain or restore the peace does not disappear because of a veto. The Charter, in Articles 10, 11 and 14, also vests in the General Assembly authority and responsibility for matters affecting international peace. The General Assembly can and should organize itself to discharge its responsibility promptly and decisively if the Security Council is prevented from acting.

To this end, the United States Delegation is placing before the Assembly a number of recommendations designed to increase the effectiveness of United Nations action against aggression.

This program will include the following proposals:

First, a provision for the calling of an emergency session of the General Assembly upon twenty-four hours' notice if the Security Council is prevented from acting upon a breach of the peace or an act of aggression.

Second, the establishment by the General Assembly of a security patrol, a peace patrol, to provide immediate and independent observation and reporting from any area in which international conflict threatens, upon the invitation or with the consent of the state visited.

Third, a plan under which each member nation would designate within its national armed forces a United Nations unit or units, to be specially trained and equipped and continuously maintained in readiness for prompt service on behalf of the United Nations. To assist in the organization, training and equipping of such units, we will suggest that a United Nations military advisor be appointed. Until such time as the forces provided for under Article 43 are made available to the United Nations, the availability of these national units will be an important step toward the development of a world-wide security system.

Fourth, the establishment by the General Assembly of a committee to study and report on means which the United Nations might use through collective action—including the use of armed force—to carry out the purposes and principles of the Charter.

The United States Delegation shall request that these proposals be added as an item to the agenda. It is the hope of our delegation that the Assembly will act on these and other suggestions which may be offered for the strengthening of our collective security system.

In so doing, we must keep clearly before the world the purpose of our collective security system, so that no one can make any mistake about it.

We need this defensive strength against further aggression in order to pass through this time of tension without catastrophe, and to reach a period when genuine negotiation may take its place as the normal means of settling disputes.

This perspective is reflected in the proposals of the Secretary-General for a twenty-year program, a perspective from which we can derive the steadiness and patience required of us.

This perspective takes into account the possibility that the Soviet Government may not be inherently and unalterably committed to standing in the way of peace, and that it may some day accept a live-and-let-live philosophy.

The Soviet leaders are realists, in some respects at least. As we succeed in building the necessary economic and defensive military strength, it will become clear to them that the non-Soviet world will neither collapse nor be dismembered piecemeal. Some modification in their aggressive policies may follow, if they then recognize that the best interests of the Soviet Union require a cooperative relationship with the outside world.

Time may have its effect. It is but thirty-three years since the overthrow of the Czarist regime in Russia. This is a short time in history. Like many other social and political movements before it, the Soviet revolution may change. In so doing, it may rid itself of the policies which now prevent the Soviet Union from living as a good neighbor with the rest of the world.

We have no assurance that this will take place. But as the United Nations strengthens its collective security system, the possibilities of this change in Soviet policy will increase. If this does not occur, the increase in our defensive strength shall be the means of ensuring our survival and protecting the essential values of our societies.

But our hope is that a strong collective security system will make genuine negotiation possible, and that this will in turn lead to a cooperative peace.

It is the first belief of the people and the Government of the United States that the United Nations will play an increasingly important role in the world during the period ahead, as we try to move safely through the present tensions.

I have already stressed the importance we attach to the United Nations as the framework of an effective system of collective security. The steps we take to strengthen our collective security are not only essential to the survival of the United Nations, but will contribute positively toward its development. The close ties of a common defense are developing an added cohesion among regional groups. This is a significant step toward a closer relationship among nations, and is part of the process of growth by which we are moving toward a larger sense of community under the United Nations.

The United States also attaches importance to the universal character of the United Nations, which enables it to serve as a point of contact between the Soviet Union and the rest of the world during this period of tension.

As our efforts to strengthen the collective security system become more and more effective, and as tensions begin to ease, we believe that the United Nations will be increasingly important as a means of facilitating and encouraging productive negotiation.

The United States is ready and will always be ready and willing to negotiate with a sincere desire to solve problems. We shall continue to hope that sometime negotiation will not be merely an occasion for propaganda.

Solving the many difficult problems in the world must, of course, be a gradual process. It will not be achieved miraculously, overnight, by a sudden dramatic gesture. It will come about step by step. We must seek to solve such problems as we can, and endure the others until they too can be solved.

Among the immediately pressing problems which require the attention of the General Assembly are the aggression against the Republic of Korea, and the problem of Formosa.

In a special and indeed a unique sense, the Republic of Korea is a responsibility of the United Nations. The actions of this Assembly, in its sessions of 1947 and 1948, outlined the United Nations aspirations for its future. Before the aggression of last June, the failure to achieve these purposes had been a matter of deep disappoinment and concern. The aggression of June 25th raised a new challenge, which was met by the stout action to which I have already referred.

I have every belief and confidence that this challenge and defiance to the authority of the United Nations will be crushed as it deserves to be, and that thereafter the future of this small and gallant country may be returned where it belongs—to the custody of its own people under the guidance of the United Nations.

From the outset, the United States has given its full support to the actions of this Assembly and of the Security Council. We shall continue to support the decisions of the United Nations as the future course of events unfolds.

We shall do our full part to maintain the impressive unity which has thus far been demonstrated in Korea.

The aggressive attack upon the Republic of Korea created the urgent necessity for the military neutralization of the island of Formosa. The President of the United States, in announcing on June 27th the measures taken to effect this neutralization, emphasized that these measures were to prevent military attack either by mainland forces against Formosa or by forces from Formosa against the mainland. The President made it clear, at that time and on several subsequent occasions, that these measures were taken without prejudice to the future political status of Formosa, and that the United States has no territorial ambitions and seeks no special position or privileges with respect to Formosa.

It is the belief of my government that the problem of Formosa and the nearly eight million people who inhabit it should not be settled by force or by unilateral action. We believe that the international community has a legitimate interest and concern in having this matter settled by peaceful means.

Accordingly, the United States delegation proposed that the General Assembly should direct its attention to the solution of this problem under circumstances in which all concerned and interested parties shall have a full opportunity to express their views, and under which all concerned parties will agree to refrain from the use of force while a peaceful and equitable solution is sought.

We shall therefore request that the question of Formosa be added to the agenda, as a matter of special and urgent importance.

Advances which can be made on these specific issues, and the improvement which can result from an effective collective security system, may help the United Nations to move in the direction of settlement of further disputes.

We also anticipate that, as our collective security system is strengthened, our efforts to achieve the regulation of armaments may then begin to be productive.

My country reaffirms its support of the United Nations plan for the international control of atomic energy which would effectively prohibit atomic weapons. We will continue to give sympathetic consideration to any other proposals that would be equally or more effective in accomplishing this purpose. We reaffirm our support of the efforts of the United Nations to work out the basis for effective regulation and reduction of conventional armaments and armed forces.

In talking about disarmament, we must keep one elementary point absolutely clear: that is, that the heart and core of any real disarmament is confidence that agreements are being carried out by every armed nation. No one nation can have such confidence, unless it has knowledge of the real facts in other countries. Such knowledge can come only from international controls based upon free international inspection in every country. There are no safe short-cuts.

Disarmament has been the subject of a great deal of propaganda effort, and this will doubtless continue to be the case. To those who advance various disarmament plans for propaganda purposes, the United Nations has only to ask this simple question: If you mean what you say, are you willing to take the first step? That first step is the acceptance of effective safeguards under the United Nations. There can be no other basis for disarmament. Only when every nation is willing to move into an era of open and friendly cooperation in the world community, will we begin to get genuine progress toward disarmament.

We believe nevertheless that efforts in this direction should continue, that plans should be made, and negotiations should go on. This subject is of such vital significance that no stone should be left unturned, in the hope that these efforts will someday be successful. . . .

My government is prepared to join with other member nations in making resources and personnel available. When the conflict in Korea is brought to a successful conclusion, many of the doctors, engineers and other technicians, and much of the resources now being used to support the United Nations military action, will be made available by my government to a United Nations recovery force.

I suggest that the General Assembly have the Economic and Social Council set up a United Nations recovery force to harness this great collective effort.

These measures not only will aid in restoring the people of Korea quickly to a condition of peace and independence, but they will demonstrate to the people of the world the creative and productive possibilities at the command of the United Nations.

Out of the ashes of destruction, the United Nations can help the Korean people to create a society which will have lessons in it for other people everywhere. What the United Nations will be able to do here can help set a pattern of coordinated economic and social action in other places, where the need is for development aid rather than rehabilitation.

We look forward to a time when members of the United Nations will be able to devote their energies and their resources to productive and creative activities, to the advancement of human well-being, rather than to armaments.

When the time comes that a universal collective security system enables nations to reduce their burden of armaments, we hope that other nations will join us in pledging a good part of the amount saved to such productive United Nations activities as I have described.

A world such as this, in which nations without exception work together for the well-being of all mankind, seems a very distant goal in these days of peril, but our faith in its ultimate realization illumines all that we do now.

In building a more secure and prosperous world, we must never lose sight of the basic motivation of our effort: the inherent worth of the individual human person. Our aim is to create a world in which each human being shall have the opportunity to fulfill his creative possibilities in harmony with all.

It is our hope that the relaxation in international tension, which we seek, will be accompanied by a great restoration of human liberty, where it is now lacking, and progress everywhere toward the "larger freedom."

But the safeguarding of human freedom is not a distant goal, nor a project for the future. It is a constant, immediate and urgent concern of the United Nations.

The United Nations should keep ever in mind the objectives set forth in the universal declaration of human rights, and we should press forward with the work of our distinguished Human Rights Commission.

While we are engaged in creating conditions of real peace in the world, we must always go forward under the banner of liberty. Our faith and our strength are rooted in free institutions and the rights of man.

We speak here as the representatives of governments, but we must also speak the hearts of our countrymen. We speak for people whose deep concern is whether the children are well or sick, whether there is enough food, whether the roof leaks, whether there will be peace.

But peace, for them, is not just the absence of war. The peace the world wants must be free from fear—the fear of invasion, the fear of subversion, the fear of the knock on the door at midnight. The peace the world wants must be free from want, a peace in which neighbors help each other, and together build a better life.

The peace the world wants must be a moral peace, so that the spirit of man may be free, and the barriers between the hearts and minds of men may drop away and leave men free to unite in brotherhood.

This is the task before us.

STOP BEING AFRAID [6]

HENRY CABOT LODGE, JR. [7]

Senator Henry Cabot Lodge, Jr., member of the United States delegation to the General Assembly of the United Nations, made this address,
his first major one before that group, at Lake Success, on October 28,
1950.

He took the floor before the Political and Security Committee immediately after Andrei Y. Vishinsky, Soviet Foreign Minister, had
delivered a two-hour speech of general and detailed indictment of the
United States. The latter's thesis was the familiar one that the United
States and not the Soviet government preached war propaganda. He
touched on the problems of Trieste, Germany, Austria, the Secretary
Generalship, atomic control, and other topics under dispute, and in each
case resorted to language that created a climate of high hostility.

Senator Lodge's reply was unusual in that he was brief (sixteen
minutes), simple, and free from diplomatic cliches. His tones and
expressions were those of conversation. But the unmistakable manliness
of his discourse apparently struck home and discomfited Vishinsky—if
we believe the pro-American observers of that incisive debate.

The junior Senator from Massachusetts, who interrupted his career
in the Senate for a period of military service in World War II, has
grown steadily in leadership and speaking ability since his entrance
into public life. In contrast to his grandfather, Henry Cabot Lodge, who
helped wreck Woodrow Wilson's League of Nations program in 1919,
the younger Lodge has a record of strong internationalism. Both by his
independent thinking and his vigorous delivery, he has become one of
the younger coterie of superior Senate speakers. [8]

I realize that the hour is getting late, and I shall not detain
the committee very long. I do want to say at the outset that
this is the first time that I have ever served as a representative
to the United Nations, and I want, first of all, to say how
honored I am to be serving here in this assemblage of distinguished men from all over the world. Perhaps because this is
my first time, my impressions may be typical of those of the

[6] Text furnished by Henry Cabot Lodge, Jr., with his permission to reprint.
For text see also *Atlantic Monthly*. 87:58-60. March 1951. Reprinted from
Congressional Record 96:A.7764-5. November 28, 1950 (daily edition).

[7] For biographical note, see Appendix.

[8] Cf. *Representative American Speeches: 1942-1943*, p116-30.

everyday citizen. It is certainly as an everyday citizen and not as an expert that I speak.

Of course, you can understand that during the past years I have read carefully the accounts of previous sessions, and I expected, therefore, when I came here to hear my country accused of being a capitalist-dominated, crude, and illegal gang of warmongers. But to expect to hear these things and to have read them in print is one thing, and actually to sit here and hear these things said is a very different thing.

I have spent substantially all of my life in the United States. I have traveled some. I have been overseas during the war, but for twenty-five years I have been active in journalism and in American politics, and all I can say is that the things I have heard said here today and during the last few days about the United States are just completely belied by my own experience.

Let me give examples of a few statements which struck me. I heard the representative of the Soviet Union (Mr. Vishinsky) say—this was three or four days ago—that he wants peace and understanding with the United States. But when you think, if only for one minute, of the insults which he saw fit to heap on the United States and the way in which he impugns and questions our motives, you cannot honestly believe that his speech was the speech of a man who really wanted peace. No one who really wants peace with someone else begins by insulting him.

Then he said—and I think I am quoting him accurately—that "force is the foundation of the American foreign policy." Yet he knows perfectly well that the United States at the end of hostilities in 1945 not merely demobilized but actually disintegrated its armed forces—and you all know that—thereby, incidentally, facilitating the territorial expansion of the Soviet Union, which is without precedent in all our human history. That is just as clear as the blue in the United Nations flag.

He spoke today of the use of Japanese troops in Korea, which I sincerely believe to be without any foundation whatever. I do not think he can produce proof of it.

Then I heard the representative of the Soviet Union and his colleague from Poland—Mr. Wierblowski—speak with a lump in their collective throats of the horror of the atomic bomb—

which is certainly very true and very real—without ever uttering a word about the horrors of being stuck in the stomach with a bayonet or of being shot by a rifle bullet, or by an artillery shell, or of being overrun by a tank. I heard not a word about the horrors of drowning because your ship had been torpedoed by a submarine. Not even a syllable was uttered about the terrors of the concentration camp and the unspeakable slavery of a police state.

I also heard some interesting figures about the United States preparedness effort. We have a saying in the United States that there are lies and lies and statistics, and you can prove almost anything you want to by figures. If you want to take United States appropriations for military purposes as a percentage of the federal budget, you can make it look very big. I think that if you take the percentage which the United States preparedness effort is of the per capita income of the everyday citizen, which is what he lives by, I think you will find that that is a much smaller percentage than is the case in the Soviet Union. I am quoting from memory now, but I think I could prove it accurately and will be glad to do so later: that about 5 per cent of the per capita income of United States citizens goes into military expenses, and I think the corresponding figure is about 14 per cent in the case of the Soviet Union.

But let us forget about those statistics because they are not what matters when one considers military affairs. What matters of course is not the dollars or the rubles; it is the military power. And everyone in this room knows that even if this preparedness effort that the free nations are engaged in attains its maximum potential way beyond what is planned—that even then it could never have any offensive capabilities against the Soviet Union. Every child knows that.

I heard the Soviet Union representative say that the Berlin railway strike of May and June 1949 was inspired by the United States. I understand that this strike was inspired by nobody other than the 16,000 strikers themselves who had a legitimate wage grievance. They were workers who lived in the western sector of Berlin but who were paid in East German marks. This currency was no good to them in west Berlin, and they asked to have their wages paid to them in west Berlin marks. The Berlin railway system, as you know, is controlled from the Soviet sector of the city. From what I am told, the Soviet Union authorities refused this demand of the workers, and the workers went out on strike. I do not suppose it is surprising that those who come from countries which do not permit workers to strike should blame the United States for starting a legitimate wage dispute. The fact is that the strike was eventually settled on the basis of a United States formula which guaranteed the workers payment in West German marks. That is just an illustration of what I have in mind by accuracy.

Then, I heard both the Soviet Union and the Polish representative speak of America as monopolistic, when actually, one of the great basic economic facts about America—and that is something which you can all verify for yourselves—is that it is a competitive country in which monopoly is actually against the law. If I were to choose one word with which to describe our American economy, I would use "competitive" rather than "capitalistic." I do not deny that occasionally Americans, like all human beings, do seek to prevent competition; but in this country, when you try to prevent competition you know you are doing something illegal and will be punished if caught.

Now I know that we in the United States are not perfect. Perhaps I can tell the representatives of the Soviet Union and Poland things that are right in the United States and more things that are wrong than they know about. But in this country we are working all the time to improve conditions, and I know we have made progress.

I have cited just a few examples of some of the statements which have been made in this committee. The men who made these statements appear to be normal men who obviously must know that these particular statements to which I have just referred are absurd. It would be easy and perhaps natural, therefore, for me to dismiss these speeches as merely a cynical and insincere collection of deliberate lies. But I do not do that.

The strange thing is that I think the spokesmen of the Soviet Union and Poland and the Ukrainian S. S. R. (Mr. Boranofsky) actually believe parts of that strange grab bag of news clippings about the United States, from which they quote so constantly. I saw the Polish representative waving a copy of an American magazine here a few days ago which contained an article which happened to suit the argument that he was making at that time. He did so with an expression of triumph on his face. I think his sensation of triumph was genuine and real for the simple reason that he does not understand what it is like to live in a country where there is free speech. If that magazine had appeared in his country, I suppose its statements would have had the consent of the government. But in our country the magazine simply represents the editor's opinion, and most Americans take full advantage of the privilege of disagreeing with the editor. In fact, the editor very often disagrees with the owner and the man who wrote the article disagrees with the editor and the reader disagrees with the man who wrote the article.

That is the way it is over here. We are a talkative people. We talk all the time. Perhaps we talk too much for our own good. But to pick out something which someone has said in Tampa, Florida, or out in Iowa, or anywhere else, and to say that that represents the United States of America is just fanciful.

I think that some of you representatives from the Soviet Union and Poland and the Ukrainian S. S. R. really believe that we are monopolistic. You believe it because you come from the world's greatest monopoly, and you just cannot imagine anything else. You also have a Politburo in which power is concentrated in just a dozen men, and you just cannot believe that power is so diffused in this country as it actually is. I believe that the ridiculous fairy tales about domination springs from the simple fact that you live in a dominated society and therefore cannot conceive of a society which is not dominated by somebody. You keep looking around all the time to see who is dominating this country. Well, there is no one.

You have made me wonder—and I say this in all sincerity—during the last few days whether you are not really frightened. Maybe you are frightened of us. Maybe you are frightened of the plain people in your own country. But I know that a frightened man can be dangerous. I am sorry there is fright, and I hope and believe that the time will come when fear will disappear, and that that time will not be far off.

I read recently in former Prime Minister Churchill's memoirs that when Mr. Molotov came to stay at Mr. Churchill's official residence during the war he had a pistol beside his bed at all times. Well, there is a certain amount of fear in all countries and in most individuals; but in many nations which are represented here—notably those nations composed of people who value their freedom—fear is not the prime motive of those who hold responsible positions.

Obviously the policies which you advocate here would be very bad for the world if it should happen to adopt them. But I cannot see how, in the long run, these policies will help the people in your own countries. The people of your countries need friends; every man needs friends. They need friends in the outside world, just as the people of our country and of all countries need friends. Now, I have been here since September 18, and I have talked with many earnest, idealistic, and sincere men and women—some of them in this room—who represent many different countries and who would sincerely like to have an efficient working arrangement with the Russian people. But you have rebuffed them; you have turned them down; you have made it impossible for people who would like to do so to cooperate with you. Your policies are certainly unpredictable, and there may be some tactical advantage in that fact, but I cannot think that the alienation of friends throughout the world is intelligent.

You may be here as members of the United Nations in a purely cynical spirit, so that you can destroy it from within and thus promote your own form of world government. I get the extraordinary impression, however, of a mixture of the conspiratorial and the childish.

As to whether all this helps your own ruling class, I cannot judge.

I believe it is unquestionably bad for the long-range interests of the everyday men, women, and children of the Soviet Union, Poland, and other countries which are now in similar circumstances.

I am confident that the condition which exists in the world is not going to last much longer, because the people of the free world whom you have finally aroused will, in a completely peaceful and orderly way, and within a very few years, create a quiet and peaceful world in which disputes will be settled by negotiation and other peaceful methods set forth in the Charter, rather than by the threat or use of force. I think that time is coming.

We hope the day will come when the oppression of religion in the Soviet Union will stop; when the creative energies of that brilliant and gifted Russian people will be released; when the Russian people will be able to mingle freely with people of other lands; and when the people of the rest of Europe will no longer live in terror of the Red army.

My advice is: Stop being afraid.

There has been some talk here of the great powers versus the small powers. We Americans are not a great power in the sense that we like power or that we have sought it. We are essentially little people whose ancestors came here from countries where they had been oppressed, so that they could get away from power politics and live quiet lives of their own. We are becoming powerful, but we are not going to use that power as some others have used it in the past. We will use it, with the other peace-loving nations, to create permanent peace, and, whether the dictators like it or not, that will be a blessing to all of suffering humanity, both in and out of the free world.

FOREIGN POLICY

OUR NATIONAL POLICIES IN THIS CRISIS [1]

HERBERT HOOVER [2]

Mr. Herbert Hoover gave this address on Wednesday, December 20, 1950, at 8:00 P.M., over the Mutual Broadcasting System.

His speech was a part of the continuing debate, touched off soon after the November elections of 1950, on the question of what should be our military-economic policy with respect to Russia. More specifically the issue was, should the United States continue to endorse the Truman-Acheson policy of resisting Russia by giving substantial military-economic support to the anti-Russian nations, or should we withdraw our military and economic forces to a Western Hemisphere "Gibraltar"—with Britain, Japan, Formosa, and the Philippines on the perimeter?

The background of the debate involved the Administration foreign policy since 1945—of participation in the United Nations, the Truman Doctrine with respect to Germany and Europe, the Marshall Plan, the Atlantic Pact, and, more recently, the Far Eastern and especially the Korean policy. The extreme reverses in Korea, our retreat toward the Pusan beachhead in late 1950, bitter outpourings by the Communist Chinese delegation before the United Nations, and the large and increasing casualty lists, the obvious weakness of the American military machine, the apparent hesitancy of Western Europe to prepare vigorously against the Russians—all explained the rising tide of American criticism of the Administration policy.

The issues implied or discussed in the Hoover analysis included: Did Western Europe have the will to resist communism? Even if the will were there, could those nations, at this late day, assemble a military machine, sufficient to guarantee successful resistance? Behind this line of inquiry was a more direct military question: Could the Russians and their puppets be militarily defeated in Europe or Asia? A third issue was: Could this nation, by withdrawing to a more limited Western Hemisphere line, successfully arm itself and ward off a Russian invasion? Still another issue was: Would the Truman foreign policy of economic and military commitments wreck our economic strength and so make inevitable military defeat?

[1] Text furnished through the courtesy of Mr. Herbert Hoover.
[2] For biographical note, see Appendix.

This Hoover argument, as usual, was well organized, concrete and factual, convincing if the assumptions were accepted, and framed in language which was extremely clear, without rhetorical complexity or embellishment. The speaker read his paper with force and with unmistakable challenge in every inflection. He was continuing his one-man campaign begun several months before on foreign policy. Although he is no supreme orator, he continued to speak in 1950-51 with much intellectual force and with considerable shrewdness; his intellectual honesty and sincerity are unquestioned.

The immediate result of the speech was a nation-wide discussion, reminiscent of the isolation-intervention debate of the late 1930's. Hoover, despite his clear disclaimer, was pigeonholed in the camp of "isolationists, 1950 brand." A large following, including the traditional nationalists, endorsed his arguments. John Foster Dulles, Wayne Morse, Thomas Dewey and other prominent Republicans argued stoutly the reverse. The party was widely split on the issue.

Assumptions in the Hoover speech to be examined by critics were: (1) Had Western Europe demonstrated its acceptance of the principle of equal sacrifice in the defense of that area? (2) Was Korea a fair analogy as a basis for inferring that American power would fail in Germany? (3) Would several American divisions in Germany have a better chance to retreat without disaster than would the divisions at present there? (4) Did the commitments made by the United Nations bind us to help defend Western Europe? (5) Was the best way of dealing with Western Europe to bargain with these nations, division for division?

Many students of these debates of late 1950 and early 1951 called for out-and-out discussion of the problems. Should the atomic bomb be immediately used against the Soviet Union? Should we risk the possible losses in Europe rather than avoid taking such chances and so "hand our enemy the greatest victory in history?" Should we acknowledge the existence of war with Red China and proceed on that basis? [3]

My fellow Americans: I have received hundreds of requests that I appraise the present situation and give my conclusions as to our national policies.

I speak with a deep sense of responsibility. And I speak tonight under the anxieties of every American for the nations' sons who are fighting and dying on a mission of peace and the honor of our country.

No appraisal of the world situation can be final in an unstable world. However, to find our national path we must con-

[3] For further comment on Hoover as a speaker, see *Representative American Speeches: 1948-49*, p89-95; *1940-41*, p196-208; *1937-38*, p80-96.

stantly reexamine where we have arrived and at times revise our direction.

I do not propose to traverse the disastrous road by which we reached this point.

We may first survey the global military situation. There is today only one center of aggression on the earth. That is the Communist-controlled Asian-European land mass of 800 million people. They have probably over 300 trained and equipped combat divisions with over 30 thousand tanks, 10 thousand tactical planes and further large reserves they can put in action in 90 days. But they are not a great seapower. Their long range airpower is limited. This congeries of over 30 different races will some day go to pieces. But in the meantime they furnish unlimited cannon fodder.

Facing this menace on the Eastern front there are about 100 million non-Communist island peoples in Japan, Formosa, the Philippines and Korea. Aside from Korea, which I discuss later, they have probably only 12 effective combat divisions with practically no tanks, air or navy.

Facing this land mass on the South are the Indies and the Middle East of about 600 million non-Communist peoples. There are about 150 million further non-Communist peoples in North Africa and Latin America. Except Turkey and Formosa, these 850 million non-Communist people have little military force which they would or could spare. But they could contribute vital economic and moral strength.

Facing this menace on the Continental European front there are about 160 million further non-Communist people who, excluding Spain, have less than 20 combat divisions now available, few tanks and little air or naval force. And their will to defend themselves is feeble and their disunities are manifest.

Of importance in military weight at this moment there is the British Commonwealth of 150 million people, with probably 30 combat divisions under arms, a superior navy, considerable air force and a few tanks.

And there are 150 million people in the United States preparing 3.5 million men into a gigantic air force and navy, with about 30 equipped combat divisions.

Thus there are 1 billion non-Communist people in the world of whom today only about 320 million have any military potency.

If we weigh these military forces as they stand today we must arrive at certain basic conclusions.

a. We must face the fact that to commit the sparse ground forces of the non-Communist nations into a land war against this Communist land mass would be a war without victory, a war without a successful political terminal.

The Germans failed with a magnificent army of 240 combat divisions and with powerful air and tank forces. That compares with only 60 divisions proposed today for the North Atlantic Pact Nations.

Even were Western Europe armed far beyond any contemplated program, we could never reach Moscow.

Therefore any attempt to make war on the Communist mass by land invasion, through the quicksands of China, India or Western Europe is sheer folly. That would be the graveyard of millions of American boys and would end in the exhaustion of this Gibraltar of Western Civilization.

b. Equally, we Americans alone with sea and airpower can so control the Atlantic and Pacific Oceans that there can be no possible invasion of the Western Hemisphere by Communist armies. They can no more reach Washington in force than we can reach Moscow.

c. In this military connection we must realize the fact that the Atomic Bomb is a far less dominant weapon than it was once thought to be.

d. It is obvious that the United Nations have been defeated in Korea by the aggression of Communist China. There are no available forces in the world to repel them.

Even if we sacrifice more American boys to hold a bridgehead, we know we shall not succeed at the present time in the mission given to us by the 50 members of the United Nations.

We may explore our American situation still further. The 150 million American people are already economically strained by government expenditures. It must not be forgotten that we are carrying huge burdens from previous wars including obligations to veterans and $260 billions of bond and currency issues from those wars. In the fiscal year 1952, federal and local expenditures are likely to exceed $90 billions. That is more than our total savings. We must finance huge deficits by further government issues. Inflation is already moving. The dollar has in six months fallen 15 or 20 per cent in purchasing power. But we might with stern measures avoid the economic disintegration of such a load for a very few years. If we continue long on this road the one center of resistance in the world will collapse in economic disaster.

We may also appraise the diplomatic front. Our great hope was in the United Nations. We have witnessed the sabotage of its primary purpose of preserving peace. It has been, down to last week, a forum for continuous smear on our honor, our ideals and our purposes.

It did stiffen up against raw aggression last July in Korea. But in its call for that military action, America had to furnish over 90 per cent of the foreign forces and suffer over 90 per cent of their dead and injured. That effort now comes at least to a measurable military defeat by the aggression of Communist hordes.

Whether or not the United Nations is to have a moral defeat and suffer the collapse of its whole moral stature now depends on whether it has the courage to (a) declare Communist China an aggressor; (b) refuse admission of this aggressor to its membership; (c) demand that each member of the United Nations cease to furnish or transport supplies of any kind to Communist China that can aid in their military operations. Such a course honestly carried out by the non-Communist nations is not economic sanctions nor does it require military actions. But it would constitute a great pressure for rectitude. (d) For once, pass a resolution condemning the infamous lies about the United States. Any course short of such action is appeasement.

And now I come to where we should go from here. Two months ago I suggested a tentative alternate policy for the United States. It received a favorable reception from the large majority of our press.

Since then the crisis in the world has become even more acute. It is clear that the United Nations are defeated in Korea. It is also clear that other non-Communist nations did not or could not substantially respond to the United Nations call for arms to Korea. It is clear the United Nations cannot mobilize substantial military forces. It is clear Continental Europe has not in the three years of our aid developed that unity of purpose, and that will power necessary for its own defense. It is clear that our British friends are flirting with appeasement of Communist China. It is clear that the United Nations is in a fog of debate and indecision on whether to appease or not to appease.

In expansion of my proposals of two months ago, I now propose certain principles and action.

First, the foundation of our national policies must be to preserve for the world this Western Hemisphere Gibraltar of Western Civilization.

Second, we can, without any measure of doubt, with our own air and naval forces, hold the Atlantic and Pacific Oceans with one frontier on Britain (if she wishes to cooperate); the other, on Japan, Formosa and the Philippines. We can hold open the sea lanes for our supplies.

And I devoutly hope that a maximum of cooperation can be established between the British Commonwealth and ourselves.

Third, to do this we should arm our air and naval forces to the teeth. We have little need for large armies unless we are going to Europe or China. We should give Japan her independence and aid her in arms to defend herself. We should stiffen the defenses of our Pacific frontier in Formosa and the Philippines. We can protect this island chain by our sea and airpower.

Fourth, we could, after initial outlays for more air and navy equipment, greatly reduce our expenditures, balance our budget and free ourselves from the dangers of inflation and economic degeneration.

Fifth, if we toil and sacrifice as the President has so well asked, we can continue aid to the hungry of the world. Out of our productivity, we can give aid to other nations when they have already displayed spirit and strength in defense against communism. We have the stern duty to work and sacrifice to do it.

Sixth, we should have none of appeasement. Morally there is no appeasement of communism. Appeasement contains more dangers than Dunkirks. We want no more Teherans and no more Yaltas. We can retrieve a battle but we cannot retrieve an appeasement. We are grateful that President Truman has denounced such a course.

Seventh, we are not blind to the need to preserve Western civilization on the continent of Europe or to our cultural and religious ties to it. But the prime obligation of defense of Western continental Europe rests upon the nations of Europe. The test is whether they have the spiritual force, the will and acceptance of unity among them by their own volition. America cannot create their spiritual forces; we cannot buy them with money.

You can search all the history of mankind and there is no parallel to the effort and sacrifice we have made to elevate their spirit and to achieve their unity.

To this date it has failed. Their minds are confused with fears and disunities. They exclude Spain, although she has the will and means to fight. They higgle with Germany, although she is their frontier. They vacillate in the belief that they are in little danger and the hope to avoid again being a theatre of war. And Karl Marx has added to their confusions. They still suffer from battle shock. Their highly organized Communist parties are a menace that we must not ignore.

In both World War I and World War II (including West Germany) those nations placed more than 250 trained and equipped combat divisions in the field within 60 days with strong air and naval forces. They have more manpower and more productive capacity today than in either one of those wars. To warrant our further aid they should show they have spiritual strength and unity to avail themselves of their own resources. But it must be far more than pacts, conferences, paper promises and declarations. Today it must express itself in organized and equipped combat divisions of such huge numbers as would erect a sure dam against the Red flood. And that before we land another man or another dollar on their shores. Otherwise we shall be inviting another Korea. That would be a calamity to Europe as well as to us.

Our policy in this quarter of the world should be confined to a period of watchful waiting before we take on any commitments.

There is a proper urge in all Americans for unity in troubled times. But unless unity is based on right principles and right action it is a vain and dangerous thing.

Honest difference of views and honest debate are not disunity. They are the vital process of policy making among free men.

A right, a specific, an open foreign policy must be formulated which gives confidence in our own security before we can get behind it.

American eyes should now be opened to these hordes in Asia.

These policies I have suggested would be no isolationism. Indeed they are the opposite. They would avoid rash involvement of our military forces in hopeless campaigns. They do not relieve us of working to our utmost. They would preserve a stronghold of Christian civilization in the world against any peradventure.

With the policies I have outlined, even without Europe, Americans have no reason for hysteria or loss of confidence in our security or our future. And in American security rests the future security of all mankind.

It would be an uneasy peace but we could carry it on with these policies indefinitely even if the Communists should attack our lines on the seas.

We can hope that in time the more than a billion of other non-Communist peoples of the world will rise to their dangers.

We can hope that somtime the evils of communism and the crumbling of their racial controls will bring their own disintegration. It is a remote consolation, but twice before in world history Asiatic hordes have swept over a large part of the world and their racial dissensions dissolved their empires.

Our people have braved difficult and distressing situations in these three centuries we have been on this continent. We have faced our troubles without fear and we have not failed.

We shall not fail in this, even if we have to stand alone. But we need to realize the whole truth and gird ourselves for troubled times. The truth is ugly. We face it with prayer and courage. The Almighty is on our side.

UNITED FRONT AGAINST RED AGGRESSION [4]

John Foster Dulles [5]

John Foster Dulles, Republican adviser to Dean Acheson, Secretary of State, gave this address on December 29, 1950, at a dinner of the American Association for the United Nations, at the Waldorf-Astoria Hotel, New York City. The address was carried over the Mutual Broadcasting System, from 8:00 to 8:30 P.M., E.S.T.

Although Mr. Dulles had announced that he intended no "reply" to Mr. Hoover, the speech, nevertheless, was a direct refutation of the former President's major views as given in the Hoover speech of December 20. In general Dulles upheld the Administration's foreign policy and attacked vigorously the "fallacy" of the "area defense" program of Hoover. The speaker, however, criticized Truman's Korean policy and warned against involvement in other "Koreas." According to Richard Wilson, Washington Correspondent of the *Des Moines Register*, Dulles' policy "lacked the clarity and newness of the Hoover hemisphere defense plan, or the finality of the do-or-die program of the all-out interventionists."

The address was obviously attuned to his highly educated visible audience, who were obviously in full accord with his ideas. He developed his subject by a review of the historical-philosophical background, in contrast to Mr. Hoover's more concrete and contemporary handling of the issue of interventionism versus hemisphere defense. Mr. Dulles' opening section suggested Toynbee's comprehensive view of Western civilization. Dulles, however, did not neglect to cite evidence and argument. His generalizations were frequent; they reflected his interest in the philosophic view of history. His strongest conclusions were couched in understatements that carried much weight.

The formality and originality of the style, together with maturity of thinking and elevation of motive, mark the address as perhaps the strongest yet given by Mr. Dulles. At the end the audience gave the speaker a standing ovation.

At the end of the year it is our good custom to pause to think about the past so that we can better plan the future. This year and it is particularly important to do that and we should be grateful to all who, out of wisdom, experience and proven idealism, help to clarify the grave issues that confront us.

[4] Text furnished through the courtesy of John Foster Dulles.
[5] For biographical note, see Appendix.

As we look back, we need not feel despondent. Great
dangers still surround us and there are many patches of ground
fog. But once we lift our vision, so that we see the present in
the light of historical perspective, it is apparent that the last
five years have been years of achievement and that our people
have already surmounted a great peril.

Nations are like people in the sense that while they *may* die
a violent death, they are more apt to die in their beds, particularly as they grow older. The great question of our time has
been whether our Western civilization had become so old and
decadent that it was bound to pass away, giving place to the
younger, dynamic and barbarian society born out of the unholy
union of Marx's communism and Russia's imperialism.

For a thousand years our Western civilization had been
dominant in the world. It won and held that leadership on merit.
It produced spiritual, intellectual and material richness such as
the world had never known before. The fruits of Western society
were spread everywhere, and men elsewhere wanted to share
them, rather than to destroy their source.

However, a thousand years is a long time, even for a civilization, and many had come to feel that Western civilization
had run its course and had become infected with the same decay
as had rotted other great civilizations of the past. The Communists shouted that everywhere. The West, they said, could
no longer produce the vital leadership or creative acts needed
to satisfy the dissatisfied masses; only communism could do that.

With that slogan they softened up the opposition and then
moved in with terrorism, subversion and civil war to gain political
control. By those methods the Russian state and the Bolshevik
Party, working hand in hand, brought about 800 million people
under their control. That is about one third of all the people
there are. And still they were rolling on toward their announced
goal of a Communist "one world."

Who was there to stop them? Many thought that they were
unstoppable; and a band-wagon trend was getting under way.

At this critical moment heavy responsibility fell upon the
United States. We were still a relatively young nation; we had
not been devastated by war, and were on that account less

susceptible than some others to the poison that the Communist Party distills. If anyone could perhaps demonstrate the faith and works needed to rally men to the cause of human freedom, it should be the United States.

The whole world watched to see. If, at that juncture, we had sought only to save ourselves that would have been public confession that the Communists were right when they said that the West had rotted. The tide of communism would have rolled on irresistibly and we would have been encircled, isolated and finally engulfed. Only as we sought to help others could we save ourselves.

Our people responded to that challenge by a five-year record of which we can be proud. Consider these deeds:

1. We showed, by example within our own country, that social justice could be had without traveling the Communist road of violent revolution and materialism. Through graduated income and estate taxes, and social security and pension plans, our capitalistic society has come to approach more nearly than the Communist world, the ideal of production according to ability and distribution according to need.

2. Within five years the colonial system, which had become a festering sore, has been subjected to orderly liquidation. Over 550 million people have peacefully won political independence. Great Britain, as the principal colonial power, took the lead. Our own direct national contribution has been the granting of freedom to the Philippines and the discrediting of racial discrimination here at home. But in many other ways, we helped in this whole great process of building between men of different races, creeds and colors a new relationship of partnership and of equality.

3. Since the end of World War II we have provided, in loans and grants, over $40 billion for the relief of other people and the reconstruction of other lands, thereby practicing the great commandment that the strong ought to lighten the burdens of the weak.

4. We took the lead in founding the United Nations as an organization for recording the moral judgments of the world

and developing ways to put power behind those judgments so as to promote collective justice and security. This year, for the first time in all time, a world organization moved with force to halt aggression. It seemed that the hope of ages had come true. Whatever now be the disappointments, we can know that the sons of the United Nations who in Korea lay down their lives, do so for the noblest cause for which men ever died in battle. They have done the indispensable by showing that world order can be made a practicable possibility. Nothing now can stop the determination of the people to achieve solidly that goal.

Now, I do not suggest for a moment that our record is a record of perfection. Our own social changes may have gone so far as unduly to curtail incentive and self-reliance. In some cases, political independence may have been given to peoples who are so inexperienced in the ways of self-government that it will be hard for them to preserve that independence in the face of the diabolically clever apparatus of Soviet communism. Our loans and grants to others may sometimes have provided temporary relief rather than incentives to bold new creations of unity and strength. Both the United States and the United Nations may have assumed political responsibilities which they did not yet have the power to back up. Policies, themselves good, often lacked efficient and timely execution. There have been grave and perhaps unnecessary setbacks. Almost surely the free world erred in relying too much on potential power, and in not creating enough military strength in being.

There is no occasion for complacency or for whitewash. There is need to expose errors and to point the way to making better use of all the moral and material assets that our people have shown they could provide. Such constructive pressures are needed and I have been among those who sought to create them. Under our political system that is a special responsibility of the opposition party.

But whatever may have been the faults and inadequacies of leadership, our people over the past five years have wrought mightily, and not without result.

A year ago, on January 1, 1950, *Izvestia's* leading editorial welcomed the New Year with these words:

Around the USSR the camp of the fighters for peace, democracy, and socialism is growing and becoming stronger.

The forces of this camp are multiplying day by day. The camp of democracy and socialism today includes the great Soviet Union, democratic Poland, Czechoslovakia, Bulgaria, Rumania, Hungary, Albania, Northern Korea, the Mongol People's Republic, the Chinese People's Republic, the German Democratic Republic.

And the editorial concluded: "Communism is conquering, communism will triumph!"

I do not know what *Izvestia* will say next Monday in greeting to 1951. I do know that, whereas between 1945 and 1950 it was boasting new conquests at the average rate of over two nations and 150 million people a year, there are, this year, no new names of which to boast. I do not predict that we have seen the end of Soviet Communist expansion, but the free world has found the way to slow down Soviet Communist expansion by cheap methods, short of open war. That is no mean accomplishment.

Communism pitted its youth against what it thought was our decrepitude; its universal creed against what it thought was our isolationism; its revolutionary practices against what it thought was our static mood. It found, to its dismay, a people who, when under pressure, did not decompose into factionalism and frustration. Unitedly, and with unpartisan and bipartisan leadership, they joined in an outpouring of compassion, fellowship and material succor such as history has never before recorded. There is scarcely a man, woman or child in the United States who has not consciously made some sacrifice, out of the highest motives of which human beings are capable. In the process they have ennobled their own character, have given new hope and courage to millions elsewhere and have discomfited the leaders of Soviet communism.

There are defects, at top and bottom, but the broad outline is not without a certain grandeur. It is not to be belittled; nor is the mood one to be reversed.

We can rejoice in the renewal of the faith that has been the rock of our foundation and out of which have gushed healing waters. We can be confident that that faith, if sustained, assures our capacity to overcome at least one of the twin dangers which, at the end of World War II confronted us. We are not doomed to die in our beds.

So much for the past. Let us look now to the future. Have we renewed our youth like the eagle's only to be shot at in battle? That might be. That was the risk our people took when they decided not to die from the internal diseases of old age.

The leaders of Soviet communism would have preferred sickness to be the method of our passing. They have great skill in spreading malignant germs and they prefer to practice that art rather than the art of open war where their nation may have *quantitative* superiority, but has *qualitative* inferiority. Party leaders have always distrusted the army and the generals, and are reluctant to give them the power that war exacts. If they have to use any army, they would rather use someone else's.

But since it seems that the free world has gained a certain immunity to the Communist Party poison, their leaders must now decide whether to accept one of those waiting periods which Stalin has taught may from time to time be necessary in order "to buy off a powerful enemy and gain a respite" or whether to resort increasingly to open war.

The fact that the free world succeeded, to the degree it did, in slowing up Communist success by methods short of war, automatically increased the risk of war itself.

But risk is not the same as certainty. Just as we surmounted, in recent years, the primary peril of inner decay, so, in the year ahead, we must seek to surmount also the peril of full-scale foreign war. We must find effective deterrents to Russian armed aggression.

The free world starts out with certain assets which, I think we would all agree, are capable of being developed into deterrents of a general war of Russian origin. Since moral factors do not weigh heavily in the Russian scale, we are forced to think somewhat in material terms.

Our inventive, resourceful and free society has given industrial productivity far greater than that of Russia. In terms of steel, aluminum, electric power and oil, the United States has a superiority of three or four to one over Russia. That ratio of superiority would not, of course, hold if Russia could take the industrial power of the Ruhr and Western Europe and the oil of the Middle East. So long as there are impediments to that, the free world has an economic power which operates as a major deterrent to open Russian aggression, particularly if we also have the will to forego some of our pleasures and put our economic machine into creating weapons on a mass production basis.

Already, within the captive world, there are grave internal weaknesses and these could be exploited by skillful opponents. Despotism, when looked at from without, usually looks solid and formidable, whereas free societies look divided and weak. Actually, that is an optical illusion. The reality is just the opposite.

Take Russia. Out of its 200 million people, only about 6 million, or 3 per cent are members of the ruling Communist Party. The political prisoners number from 10 to 15 million, or twice the total membership of the Party. The Party itself is shot through with distrust and suspicion and there are periodic purges as between Party factions. No one, even in high authority, feels personally safe. In the case of the satellite countries, the situation is even more precarious. For example, there is much unrest on the China mainland, and in Poland and Czechoslovakia the people are forced to accept officials of Russian nationality because the Russian masters cannot find any Poles or Czechs they are willing to trust.

When a few men rule despotically 800 million, that is bound to be a vulnerable position. Many of the 800 million are sure to be sullen, resentful and eager for change. Most of the others will have been so beaten into submissiveness by the harsh discipline of the police state that they have lost all sense of personal responsibility. They could not respond to the unpredictable needs which come out of war disruptions. War can be very unkind to rulers who are despots and who have systematically destroyed the individual initiatives of their people. They know that and we can increasingly help them to see the light.

When it comes to straight military strategy, the free world seems, momentarily, in a mood of some confusion and without any agreed deterrent program.

The Soviet Union has interior lines. It has concentrated men, tanks, artillery and strategic and tactical planes around the hub of the great circle of its control. The rim starts near the North Pole, swings south along the border of Norway, Finland, Sweden, West Germany, Austria and Yugoslavia; then east along the border of Greece, Turkey, the Arab states, Iran, Afghanistan, Pakiston, India, Burma, Indochina and Malaya; then northward close to the Philippines, Formosa, Japan, Korea and Alaska. From within this vast orbit, a single will can, in secrecy, plot and act to strike any one of many nations with overwhelming force.

It may be possible, by prearranged defense, to make that attack costly, particularly where sea and airpower play a role or where, as in Western Europe, there is depth and numbers and military experience on which to draw. But with more than twenty nations strung along the 20,000 miles of Iron Curtain, it is not possible to build up static defensive forces which could make each nation impregnable to such a major and unpredictable assault as Russia could launch. To attempt this would be to have strength nowhere and bankruptcy everywhere.

That, however, does not mean that we should abandon the whole idea of collective security and merely build our own defense area with the help of such other countries as we might pick because of their capacity to be useful to us.

The whole world can be confident that the United States will not, at a moment of supreme danger, shed allies who are endangered and to whom we are bound by solemn treaty, by common heritage and by past fellowship in war and peace. I do not interpret anyone as urging this. Any nation doing that would scarcely be in a position thereafter to do much picking and choosing for its own account. It would have elected a dangerous course, for solitary defense is never impregnable. It is possible to plan, on paper, and describe in words, what it seems should be an impregnable defense, a China Wall, a Maginot Line, a Rock of Gibraltar, an Atlantic and Pacific Moat. But the mood that plans such a defense carries within itself the seeds of its own collapse. A defense that accepts encirclement quickly decomposes. That has been proved a thousand times.

A United States which could be an inactive spectator while the barbarians overran and desecrated the cradle of our Christian civilization would not be the kind of a United States which could defend itself.

Fortunately, we do not have to choose between two disastrous alternatives. It is not necessary either to spread our strength all around the world in futile attempts to create everywhere a static defense, nor need we crawl back into our own hole in the vain hope of defending ourselves against all the rest of the world. We are not so bankrupt in resourcefulness that we can find only those two choices. There are others.

Around the rim of the captive world the free world can maintain enough economic and political vigor, enough military strength and enough will to resist so that these areas cannot be cheaply conquered by subversive methods, by trumped-up "civil wars" or even by satellite attacks.

That leaves to be dealt with the possibility of full scale attack by the Soviet Union itself. As against that there is only one effective defense, for us and for others. That is the capacity to counter attack. That is the ultimate deterrent.

When I was in the Senate, working for the ratification of the North Atlantic Pact, I took the position that it did not commit the United States to the land defense of any particular area; it did commit us to action, but action of our own choosing rather than action that an aggressor could dictate to us.

In Korea, the United Nations forces suffer the grave handicap of trying to repel an aggressor within the limited area he selected for an attack, at the time he selected, and with methods of war which are dictated by the terrain and the weather he selected.

Our people have loyally, sacrificially and rightly backed this historic first attempt at organized suppression of aggression. We have done so despite the fact that this effort involves the inevitable defects of any first endeavor. But we instinctively feel that there is something wrong about the method and do not want to be committed to a series of Koreas all around the globe.

That instinct is quite sound. Against such military power as the Soviet Union can marshall, collective security depends on capacity to counterattack against the aggressor. Then there can be concerted, rather than dissipated, power, for the force that protects one protects all, and with that there is a good chance of deterring aggression.

The free world is not without power in this respect. It has a strategic air force and a stock of weapons. But total reliance should not be placed on any single form of warfare or any relatively untried type of weapon. It has naval power, and potential strength on the ground. Much more of all of this needs now to be brought into being. The arsenal of retaliation should include all forms of counterattack with maximum flexibility, mobility and the possibility of surprise. The places of assembly should be chosen, not as places to defend, but as suitable stages for launching the means of destroying the forces of aggression, if aggression occurs. The United Nations, if it shows that it has the requisite moral courage, should be given the right to determine the fact of aggression so as to insure the Charter goal of armed forces not being used save in the common interest. In such ways the idea of collective security can be given sensible and effective content.

We cannnot be sure that anything we now do will, in fact, prevent the awful catastrophe of a third world war. The final decision will be made in the Kremlin. Perhaps it has been made already. That we cannnot know. We face a period that is bound to be one of grave anxiety. But so long as the die has not been irrevocably cast for war, we must assume that righteous peace may yet be possible; and we must work with all the power that lies within us to achieve that peace.

It is not pleasant, at this holiday season, to talk about instruments of death. But events in Korea have shown that peace is not to be found in an unbalance of military power. To correct that balance is a grim necessity. But it is a necessity which also requires that we be vigilant to preserve and not relax the moral safeguards with which military power needs always to be surrounded.

We can rejoice that the United Nations forces in Asia and the North Atlantic forces in Europe are under the command of two men, General MacArthur and General Eisenhower, who have demonstrated in peace and war, that they put material values second and moral values first. That should be the mood of all people.

It is not easy to do what has to be done without whipping up emotions which are provocative of war. We must make certain that no act of ours increases the already acute danger. So let us, on the eve of this New Year, solemnly consecrate ourselves to that calm resolve which, in moments of peril, is the hallmark of true greatness.

THE BASIS OF AN AMERICAN
FOREIGN POLICY [6]

ROBERT A. TAFT [7]

Senator Robert Taft gave this speech in the United States Senate on January 5th, 1951, opening the foreign policy debate there. The speaker spent some two and a half hours delivering the speech and answering questions from his fellow Senators.

The Senator, fresh from his triumph in the Ohio 1950 election, Chairman of the Senate Republican Policy Committee, strong prospective candidate for the Republican presidential nomination in 1952, gave one of the most comprehensive speeches he had ever made on foreign affairs. He followed closely his manuscript and spoke often with accelerated, rather high-pitched, "impatient" but not irascible tones. He was cool, confident of his arguments, clear, and concrete; he gave the impression of frankness and of strong personal conviction. He attacked vigorously the Administration program since Teheran and Yalta as conducted without adequate reference to Congress or without informing that body.

Taft's speech dealt with the immediate questions that Americans everywhere were raising, and he gave concrete answers to each. Senators Paul Douglas of Illinois, William Fulbright of Arkansas, and Wayne Morse of Oregon, challenged Taft in the Senate discussion that followed.

The Ohio Senator thus presented a neatly rounded-out foreign policy. Was it basically well grounded? In February 1941, he had stated with confidence, "It is simply fantastic to suppose that there is danger of an attack on the United States by Japan." Critics of Taft in January 1951 questioned whether his assumptions, for example, that Russia would not attack Western Europe, were warranted.

Mr. President, I wish to thank the majority leader for his action in opening the floor of the Senate for debate before the President's State of the Union message. In view of the crisis in which we find ourselves today, the President may well take longer for the preparation of his message, but certainly that should not prevent discussion of vital national issues on the floor of the Senate.

[6] Text taken from *Congressional Record* (82nd Congress, 1st Session). 97:58-72. January 5, 1951 (daily edition).

[7] For biographical note, see Appendix.

During recent years a theory has developed that there shall be no criticism of the foreign policy of the administration, that any such criticism is an attack on the unity of the nation, that it gives aid and comfort to the enemy, and that it sabotages any idea of a bipartisan foreign policy for the national benefit. I venture to state that this proposition is a fallacy and a very dangerous fallacy threatening the very existence of the nation.

In very recent days we have heard appeals for unity from the administration and from its supporters. I suggest that these appeals are an attempt to cover up the past faults and failures of the administration and enable it to maintain the secrecy which has largely enveloped our foreign policy since the days of Franklin D. Roosevelt. It was a distinguished Democrat, President Woodrow Wilson, who denounced secret diplomacy and demanded open covenants openly arrived at. The administrations of President Roosevelt and President Truman have repudiated that wise democratic doctrine and assumed complete authority to make in secret the most vital decisions and commit this country to the most important and dangerous obligations. As I see it, members of Congress, and particularly members of the Senate, have a constitutional obligation to reexamine constantly and discuss the foreign policy of the United States. If we permit appeals to unity to bring an end to that criticism, we endanger not only the constitutional liberties of the country, but even its future existence.

I may say that I hope the debate will occur on the floor of the Senate. I was invited to speak over the radio tonight following the speeches by former President Hoover and Mr. Dulles, and I declined because I felt that a statement of foreign policy by a Senator ought to be made on the floor of the Senate. I think there ought to be a continuous discussion of that policy during this session of the Senate.

Certainly when policies have been determined, unity in execution is highly desirable, and in the preparation for and the conduct of war it is essential. During recent months, the Republican minority has joined in granting to the President those powers which may be necessary to deal with the situation. We have not hesitated to pass a draft law, a law granting extensive powers of economic control, and almost unlimited appropriations for the armed forces. No action of the minority can be pointed to as in any way blocking or delaying the mobilization of our resources and our armed forces. If there has been any delay in the rearming, it has been in the administrative branch of the government.

But it is part of our American system that basic elements of foreign policy shall be openly debated. It is said that such debate and the differences that may occur give aid and comfort to our possible enemies. I think that the value of such aid and comfort is grossly exaggerated. The only thing that can give real aid and comfort to the enemy is the adoption of a policy which plays into their hands as has our policy in the Far East. Such aid and comfort can only be prevented by frank criticism before such a policy is adopted.

Whatever the value of unity, it is also true that unity carried to unreasonable extremes can destroy a country. The Kaiser achieved unity in Germany. Hitler again achieved the same unity at the cost of freedom many years later. Mussolini achieved unity in Italy. The leaders of Japan through a method of so-called thought control achieved unity in Japan. In every case, policies adopted by these enforcers of unity led to the destruction of their own country. We have regarded ourselves as safe and a probable victor in every war. Today it is just as easy for us to adopt a false foreign policy leading to the destruction of our people as for any other nation to do so. The best safeguard against fatal error lies in continuous criticism and discussion to bring out the truth and develop the best program. . . .

We would be lacking in the fulfillment of our obligations and false to our oaths if we did not criticize policies which may lead to unnecessary war, policies which may wreck the internal economy of this country and vastly weaken our economic abilities through unsound taxation or inflation, policies which may commit us to obligations we are utterly unable to perform, and thus discredit us in the eyes of the world. Criticism and debate are essential if we are to maintain the constitutional liberties of this country and its democratic heritage. Under the present administration, at any rate, criticism and debate I think are essential to avoid danger and possible destruction of our nation.

The principal purpose of the foreign policy of the United States is to maintain the liberty of our people. Its purpose is not to reform the entire world or spread sweetness and light and economic prosperity to peoples who have lived and worked out their own salvation for centuries, according to their customs, and to the best of their ability. We do have an interest, of course, in the economic welfare of other nations and in the military strength of other nations, but only to the extent to which our assistance may reduce the probability of an attack on the freedom of our own people.

After liberty, peace must be the goal of our policy and of our leaders—more than it has been in recent years. In order to assure progress and happiness for our people, we must avoid war like poison, except when it is absolutely essential to protect our liberty. War not only produces pitiful human suffering and utter destruction of things worth while, but it actually may end our own liberty, certainly for the time being. From our experience in the last two world wars, it actually promotes dictatorship and totalitarian government throughout the world. It is almost as disastrous for the victor as for the vanquished. War is to be preferred only to the destruction of our liberty.

It seems to me most unwise ever to admit that war is inevitable until it has occurred, and it seems to me that today our policy and the thinking of too many Americans are based too much on the premise that war is inevitable. It is a possibility which we must face, and for which we must prepare, but the theory of a preventive war, so closely related to the acceptance of that thesis, is contrary to every American principle and every moral principle. . . .

What then should be our military policy in preparation for a possible attack by Russia on ourselves or on our allies? Our first consideration must be the defense of America. Whatever one may feel about the action of the United States in other parts of the world, no matter how much of an internationalist a man may be, he must recognize that this country is the citadel of the free world. The defense of the United States itself is, of course, the first goal of our own people, essential to protect our liberty; but it is just as important to the rest of the world that this country be not destroyed, for its destruction would mean an end to liberty everywhere and to the hope of restoring liberty where it has been lost. It seems obvious that the immediate problem of defending this country depends upon control of the sea and control of the air.

There is no question that we have the largest navy in the world, and certainly, while the British are our allies, complete control of the sea throughout the world, except as it may be hampered by Russian submarines. We have a powerful air force, but it seems to me vitally necessary that that air force be increased until we have control of the air over this country and over the oceans which surround our continent. It should be capable of expansion in time of war to secure as great control as possible over the rest of the world and over the enemy country. With our resources and with Great Britain as an ally, that is not impossible. By the end of the last war, we had practically complete control of the air over Germany and Japan, and it was the decisive factor in the winning of the war. Not only is the air force necessary for defense of America, but it is the one weapon which can damage the enemy bases from which air attacks upon us can be made, and which can drop atom bombs where they may be decisive.

The greatest question of policy before the country and before this Congress, however, relates to our undertakings in Europe. Under the general principles I have laid down, I would say that we had better commit no American troops to the European continent at this time. Some modification is required in that theory because, first, we are now occupying Germany with the obligations growing out of the Second World War, and second we have made certain promises under the Atlantic Pact, which we are bound to carry out.

It might be well first to consider just what our obligations are under the Atlantic Pact. One thing seems certain. There is no legal obligation to send American land soldiers to Europe. . . .

But it was only our military planners who discussed sending American land troops to Europe. Responsible officials of the government absolutely repudiated any idea that the Atlantic Pact contemplated any such aid. If the President in his conference with Mr. Attlee, or Secretary Acheson at Brussels, has undertaken to commit the United States to any such assistance before or during a war they are usurping the authority given by law and their program should be submitted to Congress for consideration before we become obligated. The President has no power to agree to send American troops to fight in Europe in a war between the members of the Atlantic Pact and Soviet Russia. Without authority he involved us in the Korean War. Without authority he apparently is now attempting to adopt a similar policy in Europe. This matter must be debated and determined by Congress and by the people of this country if we are to maintain any of our constitutional freedoms. I note that, at his press conference yesterday, the President asserted that he had the right to send additional troops to Europe. Technically, of course, he can send troops to occupied Germany as long as the war status is in effect. But, in fact, no more troops are needed for the occupation of Germany. In fact those already there are a heavy burden on the German people. Also we hope that soon the war status may be ended by resolution. If the President has any technical right to send American troops to Europe, certainly Congress by resolution, such as the Coudert resolution, or by restriction in the appropriation bill providing the divisions required, may finally determine the policy to be pursued. . . .

The threat of communism is real. Those who are directing its affairs are brilliant and unprincipled. America must be the leader in the battle to prevent the spread of communism and preserve the liberty of the world. In the field of military operations our strongest position is in the air and on the sea, and we should not attempt to be also a controlling power on the land. We should not be a military aggressor or give the impression of military aggression or incite a war which might otherwise never occur. Operations on the continents of Europe and Asia, if any, should be undertaken only with the greatest care and under careful limitation. We must not so extend ourselves as to threaten economic collapse or inflation, for a productive and free America is the last bastion of liberty.

And finally the policy we adopt must be approved by Congress and the people after full and free discussion. The commitment of a land army to Europe is a program never approved by Congress, into which we should not drift. The policy of secret executive agreements has brought us to danger and disaster. It threatens the liberties of our people.

FOREIGN POLICY [8]

PAUL H. DOUGLAS [9]

Senator Paul H. Douglas gave this extended speech before the Senate on January 15, 1951, a continuation of the "Great Debate" of 1950-51 on foreign policy.[10]

Senator Wayne Morse precipitated the Senate debate on December 21, 1950, in his extended reply to Mr. Hoover's speech of the previous night. On January 5th, one day after the convening of the 82nd Congress, first session, and before President Truman had delivered his State of the Union speech, Senator Robert Taft gave an extended argument that, in general, duplicated the program enunciated by Mr. Hoover. On January 11, Senators Tom Connally of Texas, Henry Cabot Lodge, Jr. of Massachusetts, William Knowland of California, and Styles Bridges of New Hampshire all disputed with vigor and facts the Taft-Hoover logic.

Paul Douglas' speech was perhaps the ablest he had to that time given in the Senate. Only the conclusion is here included. For it he had prepared extensively. During the week preceding January 15 he had worked late into the night at his address, writing and rewriting. He had already expressed his views on the subject in a series of three major speeches and three national radio forums during November and December 1950.

The prestige, experience, and speaking ability of the Illinois Senator commanded respect as he argued. He had been a college professor, nationally known economist, member of the Chicago City Council, and at fifty had enlisted as a World War II marine.

He read his address, accepting many interruptions and injecting extempore replies that demonstrated his versatility in extempore speaking. His argument, organization, and details of treatment were convincing. He analyzed carefully and clearly the essential problem: "When, at what points, how, and with whom do we prepare to defend ourselves?" One by one he analyzed the representative proposals: (1) the Administration proposal of helping Europe but not taking a clear position about China and the rest of Eastern Asia; (2) the "Gibraltar" policy of Hoover to protect America; and (3) the Protect-freedom-everywhere-we-can policy. He ably defended this third choice and outlined his specific proposals for implementing it.[11]

[8] *Congressional Record* 97:240-64, January 15, 1951 (daily edition).

[9] For biographical note, see Appendix.

[10] See Introduction to Herbert Hoover's speech, December 20, 1950, p45-6.

[11] For further comment on Paul Douglas as a speaker and for an example of his addresses see *Representative American Speeches: 1948-1949*, p179-95.

Mr. President, let us determine that our civilization is not to fall and that the ice cap of the police state shall not descend upon either of us or Western culture. If that were to happen, then the liberties which we take for granted, as the air we breathe, would disappear; men could be arrested in the middle of the night without a warrant, taken to stations of secret police, and kept there without having the right of habeas corpus; they could be sentenced without trial, condemned to death, or condemned to being worked to death in a prison camp. The ice cap of tyranny would descend over the world and with that would go control over the schools, the radio, and the churches. Those who hate war and think perhaps it is not worth while to resist would be submerged and their very children would be taken away from them.

It would be hundreds of years, perhaps many centuries, before that ice cap would melt. During that time the Western civilization of which we are proud would largely disappear. Mr. President, I think that is a far worse thing to happen to the world than physical death itself.

Civilizations such as Greece and Rome have fallen in the past, and most profound students of history believe that they fell because men lost faith in themselves and failed to meet new challenges. To Gilbert Murray, the cause of the failure of Greece and Rome was that the Greeks and the Romans lost their nerve. To Dean Inge, the failure of civilizations was caused by "resignation," which he said was "the disease from which civilizations die." Arnold Toynbee, in his recent great work on history, says that civilizations fail because of "insufficient response" to "stimuli"; and the gloomy German, Spengler, had the same version, that civilizations fall because the inner faith of a civilization wears itself out. The Communists believe that this is what will happen to us. They think the advance of history lies with them.

It lies within our power to prove them right or to prove them wrong. If we have faith in the essence of our society, namely, respect for the individual and a deep desire to improve human life, and if we translate such a faith into acts, we will survive. If we do not, we are likely to fall.

We have not sought world leadership. It has been thrust upon us by time and the mysterious workings of history. It would be far more comfortable for us all if it had never come. But it has. We cannot escape it. Whatever we as a nation do, will probably be determining.

By withdrawing, we can allow the police state to take over Europe. Asia, and virtually all of the world. If this happens, we shall be hemmed in, and our own survival will be more doubtful. For such a confession of weakness would be contagious and would prevent the free world from rallying in unity. There would be a general rush of men and countries to save themselves. The result, in my judgment, would be disaster. War of course, would be a certainty.

But if weakness is contagious, so also is courage and determination. If we really resolve to resist aggressive communism, others will rally more fully to the cause and will join with us. We may not get the support of many whom we would like to have on our side. We will get the aid of others whom in calmer times we would not wish to have. But the free world will ultimately group around us. And this non-Communist world, if it will only unite, still holds the preponderance of power. It has over twice the population of the Communist world. It has many times the industrial strength of the Communists. For the moment, it is weak in military strength at its very center. But we can repair this. Freedom can win if we and all the free peoples are united. Such determined unity can perhaps still deter the aggressors from going further and give us peace. It is confessedly a slim hope, but it is the only hope for peace.

Even if—God forbid—open struggle comes, if we are determined to preserve the faith by which we live, we can rebuild much of the damage done and free ourselves and others from the fear of tyranny. In the words of Lincoln which are as appropriate for this crisis as for that of 90 years ago, "We can nobly win or meanly lose the last, best hope of man on earth." Let us resolve to win. Let us have faith and in that faith let us act.

MILITARY DEFENSE OF THE
NORTH ATLANTIC PACT NATIONS [12]

DWIGHT D. EISENHOWER [13]

General of the Army Dwight D. Eisenhower gave this radio address to the nation, a report of his North Atlantic Pact nations tour, on Friday evening, February 2, 1951. The talk, limited to fifteen minutes, was delivered from the Pentagon, Washington, D.C. The major radio and television networks carried the message. On the next day it was rebroadcast to the various nations through the Voice of America in twenty-eight languages.

General Eisenhower, as Supreme Commander of the North Atlantic Defense Force, departed for Europe by plane on January 6th, to discover the resources which each of the North Atlantic Treaty nations "was prepared to contribute against possible Communist aggression." For twenty-one days he toured the capitals of France, Belgium, Holland, Denmark, Norway, England, Portugal, Italy, Luxembourg, Western Germany, Iceland, and Canada.

He landed at West Point on January 27 and for three days there prepared his report to the nation. On January 31 he flew to Washington and reported to the President and the Cabinet, and the next day addressed Congress in an unofficial joint meeting in the Library of Congress. His address there he gave extemporaneously with the aid of a few notes. Later in the day he appeared before the Senate Foreign Relations and Senate Armed Services Committees and underwent two hours of questioning. On February 2, he appeared at length before the Armed Forces and Foreign Affairs Committees of the House of Representatives; he then reported to a Senate Preparedness Subcommittee, and in the evening made this radio address. For two days the General thus continuously reported on his trip.

An adequate interpretation of the brief broadcast of Friday evening would call for close examination of these various preceding sessions. Eisenhower's speeches of February 2 touched upon the main issues connected with America's national defense policy as it concerned the North Atlantic nations' defense program. (1) Would the United States squander its resources in strengthening Western Europe? (2) Would these European nations make a determined effort on their own behalf? (3) Were these Allies tardy in their defense programs? Here the General gave facts to indicate otherwise. (4) What would be the German role in the defense pattern? (5) Should the American military

---

[12] Text furnished by the Office of National Defense, Washington, D.C.
[13] For biographical note, see Appendix.

contribution be determined and controlled by specific ceilings and ratios (for example, one American division for each nine European divisions)?

Despite his arduous month of travel and speechmaking and conference, the General in his broadcast spoke with much decisiveness. His television appearance was a triumph in speechmaking. He looked directly at his audience, talked without bombast but with great seriousness. He used few gestures. Occasionally, for emphasis, he slowly placed his hands, palms down, on the desk at which he sat. He never faltered. His remarks added to the confidence that the millions had in him. His prestige continued to be little short of remarkable. His recommendations thus carried immense weight.

Through February the Senate debate continued, with Taft and Wherry leading the opposition to sending more troops to Europe. Gradually the position of these anti-Truman-Acheson critics changed. All agreed that the American forces in Europe should be augmented with four divisions, for the present as Secretary of Defense George Marshall explained.

Fellow Americans: As a soldier, I have been given an Allied assignment that directly concerns the security of the free world, with special reference to the countries bordering upon the North Atlantic Ocean. I have approached the task, aiming at the good of the United States of America, conscious that a strong, solvent America is the indispensable foundation for a free world. While I have reached certain conclusions, the subject of the free world's security is so vast and complex that no man could hope to master its elements to the last critical item or, in a quarter hour, to answer all questions in his fellow citizens' minds. Consequently, though I speak to you out of deep conviction, I do so in all humility, trusting to your sympathetic consideration.

Our hope remains the achievement of peace based on understanding and forbearance, the only sure foundation for peace.

We must never lose faith that such a peace can be ultimately established. We seek such a peace and no one can honestly interpret our current modest preparations otherwise.

But we should examine the current situation fearlessly and clearly, neither shutting our eyes to obvious dangers nor permitting fear to warp our judgment. America's record and America's strength certainly should prevent hysterical apprehension of the future.

Today we are faced by an aggressive imperialism that has more than once announced its implacable hostility to free government. Therefore, we strive to erect a wall of security for the free world behind which free institutions can live. That wall must be maintained until communistic imperialism dies of its own inherent evils.

One of the great questions before us is the will and capacity of Europe to cooperate effectively in this aim. Unless there exists in Europe a will to defend itself, no amount of outside help can possibly make it secure. A nation's defense must spring from its own soul; and the soul cannot be imported.

For years we have heard that Western Europe is plagued, confused, and divided far more seriously than we are; we have heard that in their homes, in factories, on the street, millions of honest workmen are daily subjected to Communist bullying; that their days and nights are haunted by the specter of invading hordes whom they cannot hope to equal in numbers or physical strength.

Furthermore, the discouragement, destruction and confusion visited upon the peoples of Europe by two World Wars sapped their productive capacity and, in some instances, reduced them to levels of near-starvation. More than this—their spirit was smothered in war-weariness.

That is a story often told. It it were the whole story, then all I could honestly do would be to recommend that we abandon the NATO Treaty and—by ourselves—attempt, however futilely, to build a separate fortress against threatening aggression. Two striking facts make such a recommendation, for me, impossible.

The first fact is that the utter hopelessness of the alternative requires our participation in European defense. We can all understand that America must be strong in air and seapower. These elements are vitally essential to the defense of the free world and it is through them that we protect the approaches to our homeland and the routes of commerce necessary to our existence.

But this alone is not enough. Our ships will not long sail the seas, nor our planes fly the world airways, if we stand aside in fancied security while an aggressive imperialism sweeps over areas of the earth with which our own future is inseparably linked.

Western Europe is the cradle of our civilization; from her originally we drew our strength, genius, and culture. But our concern in Europe is far more than sentimental. Our own security is directly involved. Europe is a highly developed industrial complex with the largest and most varied pool of skilled labor on earth. This huge potential would be a rich prize for a totalitarian invasion. Its direct importance to us is the stark fact that its possession by communistic forces would give them opportunity to develop a preponderance of power. Even this disaster would not tell the whole story.

If Western Europe should be overrun by communism, many economically dependent areas in Africa and the Middle East would be affected by the debacle. Southeastern Asia would probably soon be lost. Thus, we would be cut off from the raw materials of all these regions—materials that we need for existence. World destiny would then be dictated by imperialistic powers whose avowed purpose is the destruction of freedom.

The second fact bearing upon our participation in European defense is that the people of Europe are not spiritually bankrupt, despite the validity of many pessimistic reports. Great sections of its population have for years labored on and fought the creeping paralysis of communism. Now, the North Atlantic Treaty has brought new fuel to the flames of hope in Europe. It has noticeably lifted morale, the fundamental element in this whole situation—the force which powers all human progress.

In every capital, there is growing a desire to cooperate in this mutual security effort. All the governments that I have recently visited agreed that their defense programs must be stepped up despite economic and other difficulties—in spite of preoccupations that constitute abnormal drains upon particular nations. For example, France now wages a relentless and costly war against communism in Indo-China. Britain, still existing on an austerity level, shoulders heavy burdens in Malaya. However much those nations may differ from us in their diplomatic thinking with respect to Asiatic states, there is no question concerning their solidarity in opposing communistic aggression.

They and others on the continent, are taking measures to effect substantial increases in their defense establishments. Within the past few days, Britain has stepped up drastically its rate of preparation. The new military service program in France bars all exemptions, of every kind whatsoever. The Norwegians impressed me with their unshakable determination that never again will they be victims of occupation. To them, a fighting resistance, even to their own destruction, is preferable. And in Italy, there are unmistakable signs of a stiffening courage and determination. The same is true of Belgium, Holland, Denmark, Portugal, Luxembourg, and Iceland.

In every country, I saw heartening evidence of a regeneration in Europe's spirit. Its morale, its will to fight, will grow with every accretion to physical strength. The arrival in Europe of new American land and air units, though modest in protective influence by themselves will certainly produce added confidence and accelerate the production of military force throughout the member nations.

The European nations must, of course, produce and maintain the great bulk of the land forces necessary to their defense. For this purpose the most immediate need of Europe is munitions and equipment. Everyone of the continental nations I visited can rapidly and markedly increase its resistance power if it can be promptly furnished additional supplies of this kind. To fill this need, our loyal neighbor, Canada, with Britain and others, is shouldering part of the load.

In military potential, the free nations have everything they need—natural resources, industrial genius, productive capacity, and great reservoirs of leadership ability. Given the ingredient of morale—the determination to combine for mutual protection —the military strength necessary will be produced at a speedy pace. With every increase in strength, there will be an upward thrust in morale, resulting in an ever-mounting spiral of confidence and security.

With respect to time, no man can know at what hour, if ever, our defensive organization may be put to the ultimate test. Because our purpose is entirely defensive, we must be ready at the earliest possible moment. Only an aggressor could name the day and hour of attack. Our current mobilization, properly adjusted to our peaceful security needs, should be as rapid as any required by the emergency of war.

To you, the people of America, I repeat—as I have to the Congress and to the President—that I believe:

First, the preservation of free America requires our participation in the defense of Western Europe.

Second, success is attainable. Given unity in spirit and action, the job can be done.

Third, while the transfer to Europe of American military units is essential, our major and special contribution should be in the field of munitions and equipment.

By no means do I believe that we Americans can support the world militarily or economically. In our own interest, we must insist upon a working partnership with every nation making the common security its task of first priority. Everyone of the member nations must realize that the success of this combined effort to preserve the peace rests as directly upon America's productive, economic, and political strength as it does on any amount of military force we can develop. Only cooperative effort by all of us can preserve for the free world a position of security, relative peace, and economic stability.

Attainment of this result is largely a matter of morale and the human spirit. The free world now must prove itself worthy of its own past.

If Frenchmen can rise to the heights their fathers achieved at Verdun in 1916; if Italians can recapture the fervor of Vittorio Veneto; if the British can re-live the days of 1940 when they stood alone against Hitler; if our other allies can react to today's threat in the mode of their own revered patriots; if we here in America can match the courage and self-sacrifice of the ragged, freezing members of Washington's Army at Valley Forge; indeed, if each of us now proves himself worthy of his countrymen fighting and dying in Korea, then success is sure—a glorious success that will bring us security, confidence, tranquility.

Each of us must do his part. We cannot delay, nationally or individually, while we suspiciously scrutinize the sacrifices made by our neighbor, and through a weasling logic seek someway to avoid our own duties.

If we Americans seize the lead, we will preserve and be worthy of our own past. Our children will dwell in peace. They will dwell in freedom. They will read the history of this decade with tingling pride and, from their kinship with this generation, they will inherit more than can be expressed in millions, in acres, or in world acclaim.

It is not my place as a soldier to dwell upon the politics, the diplomacy, the particular treaty arrangements that must accompany and go forward with such an effort. But I do conceive it my duty to report from time to time, both to this government and to all others in the coalition, as to progress achieved. Thus our own and all other peoples may constantly review their decisions and plans—and, if necessary, revise them.

This evening, I come back to you only as one with some experience in war and peace, of some acquaintanceship with our friends of Western Europe, to bring you what is in my heart and mind. I shall go about my own task in this undertaking with the unshakable confidence that America will respond fully when the basic issues are understood. We know that 150 million united Americans constitute the greatest temporal force that has ever existed on God's earth. If we join in a common understanding of our country's role today and wholeheartedly devote ourselves to its discharge, the year 1951 may be recorded in our history in letters as bright as is written the year 1776.

NATIONAL MOBILIZATION

FULL ECONOMIC MOBILIZATION [1]

BERNARD BARUCH [2]

Mr. Bernard Baruch, "Elder Statesman," approaching his eighty-first birthday, gave this testimony before the Senate Banking and Currency Committee on Wednesday, July 26, 1950. The Committee was considering the Administration's bill for economic mobilization.

Mr. Baruch, reading his statement impressively and following it with a question-and-answer period, called for immediate and complete national economic mobilization, including price, wage, and rent controls and rationing. He criticized the Administration bill as inadequate to deal with the emergency growing out of the Korean war.

The Senators, listening closely and sympathetically to the man who had been Chairman of the War Industries Board in World War I and adviser to James F. Byrnes, War Mobilization Director in World War II, obviously responded favorably. Some were apparently ready to go along completely with the Baruch proposals.

In answer to the query, how should the public be sold on the proposals for rationing and economic controls, the speaker replied that Congress and the Administration lagged behind the thinking and attitude of the people. "The legislation before you," he said in the question period, "proposes that we deliberately refuse to lock the stable door until the horse is stolen."

Since the beginning of the cold war, Mr. Baruch had campaigned for the enactment of laws that would provide machinery for quickening economic mobilization. Mr. Baruch's program was finally adopted. The questions were: Would the American public cooperate sufficiently to make the program effective? Would labor continue to seek upward wage adjustments? Would the farmer, who preferred the parity system of prices, resist? Would the businessman rebel at the endless red tape (price records, for example), in prospect for him?

Mr. Baruch from his college days was a student of history. In a problematic situation he has used great energy in getting all the facts,

[1] Text furnished through the courtesy of Mr. Bernard Baruch. See Hearings before the Committee on Banking and Currency, *United States Senate, 81st Congress, Second Session*, on S.3936, Defense Production Act of 1950, July 24-26, 1950. p197ff.

[2] For biographical note, see Appendix.

proper discretion in studying them, considerable imagination as well as judgment in interpreting them and decisiveness in acting, once his judgment crystallizes.[3]

It is an honor to be asked to appear before this Committee. Events have left us no choice. We have to mobilize. Already our young men are being called. Casualty lists are coming in. The issue before us—before this Committee—is how *quickly* and how *well* is the job of mobilization to be carried out? Shall we do *now* what we know will have to be done later—and thus hasten the victory of peace? Or shall we fumble and falter and invite defeat?

The League of Nations, already dealt a near-fatal blow by the defection of the United States, was actually wrecked in 1931 when Japan invaded China and the world stood by. Had the effort to overrun Korea been ignored, the United Nations would have been wrecked. All of us—in this country and abroad—would have had to live at the point of a gun. America has taken its stand against aggression and international blackmail. Whatever the cost, I feel sure the American people will see it through —provided they are told what is expected of them and why.

If we *are* to see it through, the legislation before this committee is vital. Many parts of this bill are excellent. There is one major fault which destroys much of its value. This bill does not go far enough.

Experience has taught us that when the government steps into the market with such enormous demands requiring such quick priority, you must control all prices, including wages, rents, food and other costs, eliminate profiteering and ration certain scarce essentials. This is not a pleasant outlook. Neither is that of the young man who has to go to battle. He risks all. Those who remain at home are called upon only to have less comfort.

The situation is sufficiently grave to warrant an overall ceiling across the entire economy, overall prices, wages, rents, fees and so on, with high enough taxes to prevent profiteering and to pay all defense costs and an all-embracing, effective system of

[3] For further comment on Bernard Baruch as a speaker and example of his speeches, see *Representative American Speeches: 1945-46*, p120-31.

priorities. In urging that, I do not propose to curtail civilian production merely for the sake of curtailment· The very fact that we face a struggle of such uncertain duration and cost means that the sooner our economy is brought under control the better.

Far from being a source of hardship, the mobilization I envision would substantially strengthen this country. It would minimize the actual denials we would have to undergo. It would reduce the risks of a third world war, by serving notice to the world that our tremendous economic potential is ready to be thrown against any aggressor, if necessary. Before the peace is won, we shall have to come to this mobilization. It will never be easier to do than now.

As now drawn the bill before the committee defeats itself. This bill proposes a system of priorities over production, yet nowhere is provision made for controlling prices and other costs. Should this bill be enacted—without price control—the government may get what it wants, but with needless delay and ever-increasing prices. The public will be left to compete for the remainder—with the fattest pocketbook, not the greatest need, deciding who gets what is available. The cost of every defense item will be needlessly increased; profiteering encouraged; cruel injustice inflicted upon millions with fixed incomes or who have no pressure group to represent them. This bill, gentlemen, is an invitation to inflation.

No system of priorities can work effectively or for long, without price control. That was learned during World War I. It was forgotten and had to be learned anew, at what bitter cost, in World War II. Must we persist in repeating the mistakes of the past, even to inviting disaster? This is what I had to say on the relation of priorities to price control nine years ago, before the House Banking and Currency Committee on September 19, 1941. I quote:

Priority means giving to one before another. When this happens the man who has been displaced will seek to replace his position. If the total supply is not sufficient to go around, he will bid a higher price to get what he wants. . . . That is why government priorities cannot be wholly effective without price control. As soon as a priority is discussed—(May I emphasize this sentence) *as soon as a priority is discussed, price control must be automatically considered, too.* . . .

Much of the waste and confusion of our defense efforts today can be traced to the fact that priorities were instituted without doing the things that must go with priorities. . . .

Priorities cannot stand alone. They must be seen as a part of the whole, as one finger of the two hands needed to do the job. Along with priorities and allocations must go the elimination of profiteering; higher taxes; effective price, wage and rent controls; power to ration scarce civilian essentials where necessary; the postponement of all less essential works; a reduction of unnecessary public and private expenditures; every effort to increase production; the development of substitutes for things in short supply; control of all exports and imports; conservation of what is scarce; and an organized self-restraint among the people—the enlightened self-discipline to accept the denials which winning the peace entails.

Some may disagree when these actions should best be taken. Still, whatever action *is* taken now, must fit into a general mobilization, when, and if that becomes necessary. Surely, the least that should be done is to lay a sound foundation for the future. A system of priorities without price control is a foundation built on shifting sands.

It may be argued that the menace of inflation is not so frightful today, since we are not yet at war. Actually, the danger is greater. Today our economy already is operating at full blast, with little or no slack. Our national debt is about $257 billion, about six times what it was when Hitler invaded Poland. Living costs have climbed so high, that serious hardship already is being inflicted on many, particularly those with low or fixed incomes.

Recently, the Senate passed a bill raising all social security payments and pensions for the aged, to offset the reduction in purchasing power since 1939. These higher payments which you have voted would be nullified by your failure to enact an effective price control law.

Everywhere cities and states are searching desperately for the means of raising the salaries of teachers, firemen, policemen, nurses and others whose real wages have been so cruelly slashed by the inflation of the last ten years. How much further can our cities and states go and still avoid disaster?

The inflation of the last ten years has undermined the stability of all our colleges, churches, hospitals and other institutions, shrinking the value of endowment funds while raising operating costs.

It is forcing the reorganization of health insurance and hospitalization plans, raising the cost beyond the capacity of many to pay. It is cheapening the real worth of all insurance, all annuities, all savings. How much *more* inflation can our society stand?

Price and other controls are often opposed out of fear that such measures will concentrate power in the government and threaten our freedoms. By inclination, I, too, am opposed to government controls. But the gravest threats to the preservation of the American system today are not government controls. They are military defeat abroad and further inflation at home.

Let those who fear, as I do, too great a dependence upon government ask what could make people more dependent on government than inflation? To the extent that the value of saving is destroyed, so is the ability of individuals to care for themselves. To the extent that some are permitted to profiteer at the expense of many, the confidence of people in government and justice is sapped, leaving grievances which the politically unscrupulous can exploit.

No more effective move to achieve economy in government can be taken than to stop inflation—now. At a time like this, all postponable government expenditures should be eliminated. Each day that prices rise, the real value of every dollar appropriated by Congress shrinks. More billions will have to be voted to buy the same things; the national debt will mount needlessly.

Some contend price increases can be prevented by public appeals and threats to invoke price control legislation. That hope has already been dashed. Its fallacy lay in the fact that such threats could be effective only if price control legislation were already on the statute books, on a stand-by basis, ready to be put into instant operation.

Under such a stand-by law, with its due notice, the President would have had the legal authority to roll back the price increases of recent weeks to levels prevailing before the emergency began. The knowledge that the government had this power might have prevented these price rises.

That was one of the many reasons for my insistence over the years on the necessity for putting into law a full stand-by mobilization program—to be able to prevent the runaway price increases which a war emergency always brings. Now, we have no alternative but compulsory controls—or pay the piper of inflation.

To wait until prices have run out of hand before legislation is sought means that action will not be taken until too late, until *after* additional inflation has taken place. This legislation before you proposes that we deliberately *refuse* to lock the stable door until the horse *is* stolen.

The rise in prices which has already occurred since the Korean outbreak will be used to justify wage increases this fall and winter. Those wage increases may not do labor any good since higher wages will lead to still higher prices. Once the inflationary race has begun, it becomes ever more difficult to check. There will always be new groups to cry, "Wait with your controls until we have caught up."

The right time to stop inflation is always—*now*! It may be said that while it is true *economically* that priorities must be accompanied by price controls, it is too soon *politically*. The people aren't ready for it, so this argument runs, implying that we must wait for further disaster.

Those who believe this, misread the temper and intelligence of the American people. Who opposes price control? The millions whose savings will be reduced if inflation continues? The millions of teachers, firemen, policemen, nurses, civil servants, and others with fixed incomes? Old-age pensioners struggling on inadequate subsistence grants? Widows living on the insurance left them by their husbands? Workers who find their real wages cut by rising living costs? Farmers who find the cost of the things they must buy mounting?

Is the omission of price control legislation today but a repetition of the tragic blundering of the recent war? As you know, the price control bill finally passed by Congress in 1942 left wages to run free and allowed farm prices to rise to 110 per cent of parity. That law legalized inflation. More than a year later, when this effort to control prices in piecemeal, partial manner broke down, a crude substitute for the overall ceiling which I originally proposed was adopted. But by then a terrible price had been paid in an inflation which added a hundred billions to the cost of the war, needlessly prolonging the conflict, unnecessarily increasing the toll of dead and wounded.

Is a lack of courage to impose ceilings on wages, farm prices and profits the real reason why price controls are now being neglected? Wages, rent and food costs are the largest components of all prices. They cannot be left to run free, if inflation is to be halted. I believe that each of the major segments of society will submit to ceilings on their gains, if all are treated fairly and equitably. Under any system of price and wage control, machinery would be established for correcting inequities and for orderly changes where the needs of defense or justice required them.

Many people, I realize, still hope that the Korean crisis will pass off without upsetting ourselves too much. This is a futile, illusory hope. That doesn't mean I regard another world war inevitable. It is still possible to prevent another terrible conflict—but only through a far greater effort than has thus far been proposed.

We dare not blind ourselves to the fact that we are in a race against the enemy—and so far are lagging in that race. When the recent war ended we scuttled and ran, demobilizing before the peace was won. The Soviet Union, though, kept several million men under arms; their munitions plants continued to produce sizable quantities of military weapons. While we were stocking our homes with refrigerators and television sets, the Soviets were stocking tanks and radar. Because we permitted the Soviets to gain this head-start in their mobilization, we now face a round of puppet aggressions—where next who can tell?

More than two years ago, in testifying on the so-called Marshall Plan, I warned that the time had come to mobilize the American economy if peace was to be preserved. Had we begun to mobilize then, two years ago, the Korean invasion might never have taken place.

This lag behind the Soviet Union's mobilization for war must be reduced. Korea is not the arena of final decision. It is to the basic disparity between the advanced Soviet mobilization and the lack of mobilization on the part of the democracies that we must direct ourselves. The essence of our defense policy, I have repeatedly stressed, must be to pace ourselves *vis-a-vis* the Soviets. Even if the Korean affair did blow over, we still would have to mobilize—or invite aggression elsewhere.

How large will the necessary effort be? I do not have that information. The President has already stated that it will extend beyond the $10 billion thus far requested. In his message to Congress, the President specifically mentioned the need to step up our assistance to Western European nations in rearming themselves against possible aggression. How rapidly that program must be pushed depends on the pace of Soviet rearmament.

Nor is the effort required of us to be measured merely in terms of direct military needs. Our defensive strength reflects not only our military establishment, but innumerable other things, such as the state of our raw material stockpiles, the number of freight cars we have, the adequacy of electric power, of oil supplies, steel capacity and so on. We must develop new sources of supply or substitutes for chrome, manganese and other supplies which we must expect will be cut off in event of war.

To bring in any major expansion of plant capacity or of raw materials, takes two, three, in some cases, five years. Should war break out in two, three or five years, these deficits in our economy would be sources of weakness, which would cost us dearly in blood and treasure.

Put another way, what we do—or do not do today—will constitute sources of strength or weakness in event of war any time in the next five years. Wherever the gap between our normal civilian pursuits and what war might require is dangerously wide, steps should be taken promptly to narrow that gap.

Many of these actions will require scarce materials or limited manpower. Less essential civilian activities will have to be curtailed to free those resources. Voluntary controls cannot possibly be adequate for what needs to be done—if it is to be done in time. Only a selfish few can make voluntary controls unworkable. Voluntary controls *are* important for the transition period until the machinery of mobilization is set up.

To limit the effectiveness of our mobilization to what can be done through voluntary means is to jeopardize everything we hold dear, our liberties, our possessions, the futures of our children. Shall we risk all that—for what? To avoid petty inconveniences? For petty profit?

Perhaps I should emphasize this thought. The term "mobilization" sounds bad. It raises frightening visions of all our young men thrust into foxholes, of all sorts of hardships and regimentations at home. But "mobilization" properly done can be a source of strength.

Our aim should be to organize the nation so that every factory and farm, every man, every dollar, every bit of material can be put to use where it will strengthen our defenses and fill the most essential needs first. There should be equal treatment for all. All demands should be kept in balance, for defense abroad and for defense at home, for the needs of our civilians and for our allies.

The weight of the different elements to be kept in balance will shift with time. What I propose is that we organize ourselves—all our resources of men, money, materials, morale—so that whatever happens—new aggressions abroad, possible destruction at home—whatever happens, the armed forces can get what they need, when they need it, with the least necessary dislocation of the civilians.

This requires putting everything in readiness now—organizing all our resources into pools that can be readily tapped, passing all necessary laws now, setting up the necessary machinery of mobilization and civilian defense so that it is capable of swift expansion, and creating now, the central mobilizing agency to guide the flow of all our resources. Throughout our economy direction must replace drift. Purpose must replace aimlessness.

Abroad there would have to be another body, in continuous operation, coordinating the actions of the other United Nations who are cooperating with us in this struggle for real and lasting peace. This organization might be developed out of the existing European Recovery Program. One of its functions would be to find and tap new resources, It is not enough simply to divide existing resources. The total resources at the command of the free peoples of the world must be constantly swelled.

America, by itself, cannot save the whole world. We can only help those nations who are willing to mobilize themselves to fight aggression. There must be a common sharing of burdens. It will not do for us to incur deficits, while others store surpluses for a "rainy" day. The rainy day has come.

To sum up my recommendations:-

1. Organize America for all-out mobilization, with a general ceiling over the entire economy to prevent further inflation and an all-embracing system of priorities to strengthen our defenses and minimize dislocations.

2. The very least that must be done is to amend this priorities legislation to provide for effective price and wage control and rationing authority. To do less is to invite cruel suffering and possible disaster.

3. Taxes high enough to eliminate profiteering and to cover *all* defense costs. These taxes should take effect for at least half of this year.

4. Continued rent controls with provision for clearly justifiable increases.

5. Prompt creation of an overall mobilizing agency to synchronize all our efforts.

6. Postpone less essential expenditures. As an aid to that a Capital Issues Committee should be established under the Secretary of the Treasury to review all capital issues, public and private, deferring less essential projects to make sure housing, schools, hospitals and other more essential needs are met first.

7. Strengthen the United Nations by coordinating our efforts with it in common defense of peace.

8. Speedier assistance in the rearming of those nations ready to resist aggression, along with the expansion of our own defense forces.

Nearly three years ago I clipped an item from a newspaper which seems ominously prophetic today. It told of a boast made by a Soviet general. This general boasted that the Western democracies were bound to be defeated by the Soviet Union because they would not make the sacrifices necessary to arm themselves. They prized their standards of living too highly. They would not be willing to accept the discipline to put "guns" over "butter." In Russia, though, this general boasted, the people were inured to hardship. The Soviet government would force the sacrifices to mobilize. A lean and hungry, but mobilized Russia would overrun a Western world which couldn't bring itself to mobilize—in time.

That is the test which confronts us—not only this country but all of the free peoples of the world. It is the choice of "peace" or "butter," of mobilizing our strength now, while peace can still be saved, or of clinging to petty wants and petty profits, imperilling our freedom and our civilization.

No outside enemy can defeat us. We *can* defeat ourselves. Gentlemen, yours is the decision. Which shall it be—discomfort or defeat?

NATIONAL EMERGENCY [4]

HARRY S. TRUMAN [5]

President Harry S. Truman delivered this address on the national emergency over the radio from Washington, D.C., on December 15, 1950. He followed his Friday night message by proclaiming on December 16 a state of emergency.

This nation-wide broadcast was a move by the United States to meet the aggressive challenge of international communism. In Korea the Red Chinese and North Koreans were striking with overwhelming force to annihilate or drive into the Yellow Sea the United Nations forces. In Europe the Western nations were comparatively defenseless in the face of the massed might of Russia. In the United Nations Security Council and General Assembly, the Soviets, with the visiting Chinese Red delegates, had waged a continual war of propaganda with no sign of interest in a settlement.

The speech and next morning's proclamation were the climax of a week of presidential and Cabinet conferences with congressional leaders of both parties and with civilian advisers on mobilization. Broad agreement was reached concerning the economic and military measures proposed in the address. The proclamation served both a legal purpose (adding new powers) and a psychological one, in impressing the people with the need for the coming sacrifices.

I am talking to you tonight about what our country is up against, and what we are going to do about it.

Our homes, our nation, all the things we believe in are in great danger. This danger has been created by the rulers of the Soviet Union.

For five years we have been working for peace and justice among nations. We have helped to bring the free nations of the world together in a great movement to establish a lasting peace.

Against this movement for peace, the rulers of the Soviet Union have been waging a relentless attack. They have tried to undermine or overwhelm the free nations, one by one. They have used threats and treachery and violence.

---

[4] Text furnished by the White House.
[5] For biographical note, see Appendix.

In June, the forces of Communist imperialism broke out into open warfare in Korea. The United Nations moved to put down this act of aggression, and, by October, had all but succeeded.

Then in November, the Communists threw their Chinese armies into the battle against the free nations.

By this act, they have shown that they are now willing to push the world to the brink of a general war to get what they want. This is the real meaning of the events that have been taking place in Korea.

That is why we are in such grave danger. The future of civilization depends on what we do—on what we do now, and in the months ahead.

We have the strength and we have the courage to overcome the danger that threatens our country. We must act calmly, wisely and resolutely.

Here are the things we will do:

First, we will continue to uphold, and if necessary to defend with arms, the principles of the United Nations, the principles of freedom and justice.

Second, we will continue to work with the other free nations to strengthen our combined defenses.

Third, we will build up our own army, navy and air force and make more weapons for ourselves and our allies.

Fourth, we will expand our economy and keep it on an even keel.

Now, I want to talk to you about each one of these things.

First, we will continue to uphold the principles of the United Nations. We have no aggressive purpose. We will not use our strength for aggression. We are a tolerant and a restrained people, deeply aware of our moral responsibilities and deeply aware of the horrors of war.

We believe in settling differences by peaceful means, and we have made honest efforts to bring about disarmament. We will continue those efforts, but we cannot yield to aggression.

Though the present situation is highly dangerous, we do not believe that war is inevitable. There is no conflict between the legitimate interests of the free world and those of the Soviet

Union that cannot be settled by peaceful means. We will continue to take every honorable step we can to avoid general war.

But we will not engage in appeasement. The world learned from Munich that security cannot be bought by appeasement.

We are ready, as we have always been, to take part in efforts to reach a peaceful solution of the conflict in Korea. In fact, our representatives at Lake Success are taking part in just such efforts today.

We do not yet know whether the Chinese Communists are willing to enter into honest negotiations to settle the conflict in Korea. If negotiations are possible, we shall strive for a settlement that will make Korea a united, independent and democratic country. That is what the Korean people want, and that is what the United Nations has decided they are entitled to have.

Meanwhile our troops in Korea are continuing to do their best to uphold the United Nations. General [J. Lawton] Collins, Chief of Staff of the Army, who returned a few days ago from Korea, reported that our military forces there are well organized and well equipped. I am confident that our military forces, together with their comrades in arms from many nations, will continue to give a good account of themselves. They know they are fighting for the freedom and security of their own homes and families.

The danger we face exists not only in Korea. Therefore, the second thing we are going to do is to increase our efforts, with other free nations, to build up defenses against aggression on other parts of the world. In dealing with the Korean crisis, we are not going to ignore the danger of aggression elsewhere.

There is actual warfare in the Far East, but Europe and the rest of the world are also in great danger. The same menace— the menace of Communist aggression—threatens Europe as well as Asia.

To combat this menace, other free nations need our help, and we need theirs. We must work with a sense of real partnership and common purpose with these nations. We must stand firm with our allies, who have shown their courage and their love of freedom.

The United States, Canada and the ten nations of Western Europe who are united with us in the North Atlantic Treaty, have already begun to create combined military defenses. Secretary of State [Dean] Acheson is flying to Europe on Sunday. He and representatives of these nations will complete the arrangements for setting up a joint army, navy and air force to defend Europe. The defense of Europe is of the utmost importance to the security of the United States.

We will continue to provide assistance to European countries, and to other free countries in other parts of the world, because their defense is also important to our own defense.

The Communist rulers are trying their hardest to split the free nations apart. If they should succeed, they would do staggering damage to the cause of freedom. Unity with our allies is now, and must continue to be, the foundation of our effort.

Working together, the free nations can create military forces strong enough to convince the Communist rulers that they cannot gain by aggression.

Working together, the free nations can present the common front, backed by strength, which is necessary if we are to be in a position to negotiate successfully with the Kremlin for peaceful settlements. Working together, we hope we can prevent another world war. In order to succeed, we in our country have a big job ahead of us.

That is why the third thing we must do to meet the present danger is to step up our own defense program. We are expanding our armed forces very rapidly. We are speeding up the production of military equipment for our own armed forces and for our allies.

We have a large navy. We have a powerful air force. We have units around which a strong army can be built. But measured against the danger that confronts us, our forces are not adequate.

On June 25, when the Communists invaded the Republic of Korea, we had less than 1.5 million men and women in our army, navy and air force.

Today, our military strength has reached about 2.5 million. Our next step is to increase the number of men and women on active duty to nearly 3.5 million.

I have directed the armed forces to accomplish this as soon as possible. The army and the navy will be able to do this within a few months. It will take the air force somewhat longer. In addition to these men and women on active duty, we have about two million more in the National Guard and the Reserves who are subject to call.

As part of the process of achieving a speedier build-up, the number of men to be called up under the Selective Service System has been raised, and two additional National Guard divisions are being ordered to active duty in January.

At the same time we will have a very rapid speed-up in the production of military equipment. Within one year we will be turning out planes at five times the present rate of production. Within one year combat vehicles will be coming off the production line at four times today's rate. Within one year the rate of production of electronics equipment for defense will have multiplied four and a half times.

These will not be weapons for our own armed forces alone. They will constitute an arsenal for the defense of freedom. Out of this arsenal we will be able to send weapons to other free nations to add to what they can produce for their own defenses. And in this same arsenal we will provide a large reserve of weapons to equip additional units in our own armed forces whenever that may be necessary.

Furthermore, while we are working toward these immediate goals in manpower and equipment, we will also expand our training and production facilities so as to make possible a very rapid expansion to full mobilization if that becomes necessary.

We can handle this production program, but it will require hard work. It will require us to make a lot of changes in our ordinary ways of doing things.

And this brings me to our fourth big job. In order to build the military strength we need, we will have to expand our production greatly. We must also prevent inflation, and stabilize the cost of living.

If we are to make the weapons we need soon enough, we shall have to cut back on many lines of civilian production. But we can not build up and maintain our armed might, and the industrial strength underlying it, simply by cutting back civilian production. We must produce more—more steel, more copper, more aluminum, more electric power, more cotton, more of many other things.

We must set very high targets and be willing to make an all-out effort to reach them. Workers will be called upon to work more hours. More women, and more young people and older workers will be needed in our plants and factories. Farmers will have to set higher production goals. Business men will have to put all their know-how to work to increase production.

A defense effort of the size we must now undertake will inevitably push prices up, unless we take positive action to hold them down.

We have already taken a number of steps. We have put restrictions on credit buying. We have increased taxes. I hope that the Congress will enact an excess-profits tax at this session. Still further taxes will be needed.

We can not escape paying the cost of our military program. The more we pay by taxes now, the better we can hold prices down. I have directed that recommendations be prepared, for early submission to the Congress, to put the increased cost of defense as nearly as possible on a "pay-as-you-go" basis.

I have also instructed the Director of the Budget to reduce the nonmilitary expenditures in the new federal budget to the minimum required to give effective support to the defense effort.

The measures I have just mentioned—credit control, higher taxes and reduced nonmilitary expenditures—are essential. They are our primary defense against inflation, because they strike at the sources of inflation. But as we move into a greatly increased defense effort, we must also take direct measures to keep prices in line.

The government is starting at once to impose price controls upon a number of materials and products. These will be mainly items important to defense production and the cost of living.

In those fields where price control is imposed, the government will also undertake to stabilize wages, as the law requires.

In the immediate future, a series of control orders will be announced by the Economic Stabilization Agency.

In addition, the agency will announce fair standards for prices and wages in those cases where mandatory controls are not imposed. I ask everyone concerned not to set prices and wages higher than these standards will allow. If these standards are violated, it will speed-up the imposition of mandatory controls, including roll-backs where needed.

As we move ahead with this mobilization effort, there will be increased need for central control over the many government activities in this field. Accordingly, I am establishing an Office of Defense Mobilization. I am appointing Mr. Charles E. Wilson to be director of this office. Mr. Wilson is resigning as president of the General Electric Company to take this job.

In his new position, he will be responsible for directing all the mobilization activities of the government, including production, procurement, manpower, transportation and economic stabilization.

The government is also moving forward with preparations for civil defense. I have appointed former Governor Millard Caldwell of Florida to be Federal Civilian Defense Administrator.

In addition, I have recommended legislation to the Congress which will authorize the Federal Government to help states and cities in their civil defense preparations. I hope the Congress will enact this legislation soon, so that the civil defense work which has already started can be greatly speeded up.

These are our plans for making our country stronger.

As we go forward, we must keep clearly in mind the meaning of what we are doing. Our freedom is in danger. Sometimes we may forget just what freedom means to us. It is as close to us, as important to us, as the air we breathe. Freedom is in our homes, in our schools, in our churches. It is in our work and our government and the right to vote as we please. Those are the things that would be taken from us if communism should win.

Because our freedom is in danger we are united in its defense. Let no aggressor think we are divided. Our great strength is the loyalty and fellowship of a free people. We pull together when we are in trouble, and we do it by our own choice, not out of fear, but out of love for the great values of our American life, that we all have a share in.

In this great defense effort that we are undertaking, things may not always go as smoothly as we would wish, either in Washington or in your home town. But remember that we are building our defenses in the democratic way and not by the iron rule of dictatorship.

Those of us who work in the government will do our best. But the outcome depends, as it has always depended, on the spirit and energy of our people. The job of building a stronger America must be done on our farms, in our factories and in our homes. It must be done by every one of us, wherever we are, and whatever our jobs may be.

Our fighting men in Korea have set an example that should inspire us all. Attacked by superior numbers, and in the bitterest of winter weather, they were resolute, steady and determined. Their steadfast courage in the face of reverses is one of the most heroic stories in our country's history.

In the days ahead, each of us should measure his own efforts, his own sacrifices, by the standard of our heroic men in Korea.

Many of you who are young people will serve in the armed forces of your country. Nothing you will do later in life will be of greater benefit to your homes, your communities, or your friends.

Many others of you will have to work longer hours in factories or mines or mills. Think of this not as longer hours, but as more planes, more tanks, more ships, more of all the things that are needed for the defense of your homes and your way of life.

All of us will have to pay more taxes and do without things we like. Think of this, not as a sacrifice, but as an opportunity, an opportunity to defend the best kind of life that men have ever devised on this earth.

As I speak to you tonight, aggression has won a military advantage in Korea. We should not try to hide or explain away that fact.

By the same token, we should draw renewed courage and faith from the response of the free world to that aggression.

What the free nations have done in Korea is right, and men all over the world know that it is right. Whatever temporary setbacks there may be, the right will prevail in the end.

Because of all these things I have been talking about with you, I will issue a proclamation tomorrow morning declaring that a national emergency exists. This will call upon every citizen to put aside his personal interests for the good of our country. All of our energies must be devoted to the tasks ahead of us.

No nation has ever had a greater responsibility than ours has at this moment. We must remember that we are the leaders of the free world. We must understand that we cannot achieve peace by ourselves, but only by cooperating with other free nations and with the men and women who love freedom everywhere.

We must remember that our goal is not war but peace. Throughout the world our name stands for international justice and for a world based on the principles of law and order. We must keep it that way. We are willing to negotiate differences, but we will not yield to aggression. Appeasement of evil is not the road to peace.

The American people have always met danger with courage and determination. I am confident we will do that now, and, with God's help, we shall keep our freedom.

INTERNAL SECURITY [6]

PAUL H. DOUGLAS [7]

Senator Paul H. Douglas of Illinois gave this argument against the Internal Security Act of 1950 (the McCarran Communist-control measure), before the United States Senate, on September 9, 1950. The bill required that all Communists and Communist organizations must register with the government; in time of war emergency the government has power to hold Communists in detention camps; a large number of new restrictions were placed on immigration and naturalization. Persons who had ever belonged to a Communist organization were barred from entering the country.

Douglas objected to the bill because it would not prevent sabotage or espionage; it would lead to the smearing of innocent persons; it could lead to the labeling of good organizations as Communist fronts; it could lead to the heavy punishment of innocent persons. Only the first part of the argument is here included. The student should read the entire speech and the rest of the Senate debate on this subject.

Both houses passed this anti-subversive legislation, the President vetoed the measure, but Congress quickly overrode his protest.[8]

Mr. President, I should like to address myself to the internal security bill, S. 4037, which is known as the McCarran bill.

As members of Congress and the country proceed to discuss the bill, which is perhaps the most important bill dealing with civil liberties we have ever had before us, all thinking persons feel the tug of two separate sets of values, namely, security and freedom. In the long run, these values reinforce each other. We need our country to be secure in order that we may be internally free.

It was Abraham Lincoln, I think, who said he was saving the country in order that he might then save the Constitution. Similarly, although this is not often appreciated, true security is ultimately created by freedom and liberty. For under freedom, government is based upon mutual assent and not upon force

---

[6] *Congressional Record, 81st Congress, Second Session.* 96:14586-14605, (daily edition). September 8, 1950.

[7] For biographical note, see Appendix.

[8] For further comment on Douglas, see above, page 72.

imposed from above and consequently it is at once more lasting and can resist greater external and internal shocks. It is largely because of this combination of security and freedom, of liberty and union, as Daniel Webster referred to it, that our country has grown great in moral and in physical power and today is the unquestioned leader of the world.

But while both these principles ultimately help each other and the people of the nation, there are frequently times when they seem to come in conflict and when the problem of how to combine them is very perplexing. There are some who in the name of security would have us abandon freedom while there are others who in their zeal for liberty would disregard the needs for security.

The American people made a conscious choice in believing that liberty gave them the best chance for both personal development and national security when they forced the adoption of the Bill of Rights or the first ten amendments to the Constitution. Milton and Locke had already argued both eloquently and well for these principles and sixty years later John Stuart Mill was to develop them further. But it was our own George Mason, James Madison, and Thomas Jefferson who put into New World terms the passionate desire of farmers, mechanics, professional men, yes, and the women, too, for liberty and to restrain tyrannical governments from invading the basic freedoms of men.

We are all acquainted with the provisions of the Bill of Rights but it is well for us to remind ourselves about their concrete nature; namely, Congress is neither to establish a state church nor to forbid people from freely exercising their religious choices. It shall not abridge the right of people to assemble peacefully and to petition their government. Life, liberty, and property are not to be taken arbitrarily or without due process of law.

The people are to be secure in their homes and persons against unreasonable searches and seizures by the police. Men are not to be arrested without a warrant, cannot be held to answer for a capital crime unless they have been indicted by a grand jury, shall enjoy the right to a speedy and public trial, where the accused must be informed of the charges against them and have the right to counsel, to confront the witnesses and to produce witnesses of their own. Excessive bail is not to be required nor cruel and unusual punishments inflicted.

Those are the details of the Bill of Rights, which of course is not merely in our national Constitution, but has been incorporated in most of the state constitutions as well.

The fundamental spirit and faith behind the Bill of Rights is simple yet profound.

First. It is based upon the belief that men if given a chance to weigh the facts will in the long run be able to separate truth from error and to arrive at approximately correct conclusions and choices. Many ideas which were unpopular at a given moment have ultimately proved to have great value. I can only mention amongst these the theory that the earth moves around the sun, that there is an evolutionary process going on throughout the animal and vegetable kingdoms, that many diseases are disseminated by the spreading of bacteria, that matter is convertible into energy, and in the world of social relations that "all men have unalienable rights to life, liberty, and the pursuit of happiness." All these ideas when first advanced were bitterly disliked.

We now mention the names of Bruno, Kepler, Copernicus, Darwin, Pasteur, Einstein, Jefferson, and they are hallowed by the vindication which time has brought to them, but in the beginning these men were unpopular, and there were many who would have suppressed them, and stopped them from advancing their ideas. Efforts were made to suppress their ideas. Had this been done, the world would have suffered. After hard struggles these ideas first came to be tolerated and then in the competition of the market established their truth.

It does not, of course, follow that because virtually all beneficial movements and ideas have been originally unpopular that all unpopular ideas and movements are therefore ultimately beneficial. This does not follow at all. The number of wrong and perverted theories which have been unpopular has on the contrary probably been far greater than those which were finally beneficent. While to be great is to be misunderstood, it does not follow, either in logic or in life, that to be misunderstood is necessarily to be great.

But what these examples should do for us is to make us very chary about trying to exterminate ideas by force. It is always just possible that the idea to which we violently object may be true and helpful. If we crush it out we destroy its chance to prove its worth and we shut ourselves and our descendants off from any possible benefits which may come. Of course, we do not believe the new idea has any merit, but there is always the chance that it may.

Second. Furthermore, ideas are seldom either all good or all bad. There is likely to be at least a grain of truth in doctrines which are otherwise false. If they are completely suppressed, the true is thrown out along with the false. If the idea is allowed to be stated and is then examined, what is of value can then be separated from the false and incorporated into our life. The kernel of truth which lies in the mass of chaff is retained and taken over.

It is in large part because of this basic willingness of Americans to tolerate and to examine new ideas that we owe both our material and our spiritual progress. This is notably and admittedly the case in the field of mechanical inventions and business methods in which we lead the world. But it is also true in the field of political ideas. We were the first in the modern world to make the great experiment of popular government on a large scale. We are the true inventors of federalism. The people of other countries, such as the Swiss and the Australians, have built on our example. We have built up the most extensive and the best system of free popular education in the world, extending from the kindergarten to the university; we are giving the most scientific aid to agriculture of any country and we are harnessing great rivers in the service of man. Never in the history of the world have so many different kinds of people, with such widely differing racial and cultural backgrounds, lived together on such terms of mutual respect. Of course we still have great problems and defects, but never have a great people made such progress in so short a time. We are now furnishing the major driving power for the ideal of a peaceful world cooperating under the rule of law.

A large part of the credit for this must go to the experimental and questioning type of mind which our American institutions have encouraged and which has both created and been formed by the spirit of our Bill of Rights.

Third. But the cause for freedom of discussion goes even deeper. Although the predominant opinion may be completely true and the heretical theory absolutely false, it is better for orthodoxy to be challenged than for it to be passively accepted without questioning or examination. For truths which are not examined are not sufficiently understood and valued. It is in the conflict of ideas and under stress that men find out for themselves the bedrock truths. It is only in that way that the steel of their lives is hardened, if I may use that expression. From having been mere platitudes, these truths become fundamental realities to which one can tie.

It is for this reason perhaps that some religious groups have used the device of the "devil's advocate" so that truth might shine forth more clearly because of the opposition of error. When men have the chance to compare doctrines, if the choices are fairly presented, it is the faith of one who is a democrat, with a small "d," and, we hope, a Christian, men will overwhelmingly tend to choose correctly and in choosing they will know the reasons for their choice. The better way of action will be more firmly fixed in their minds and hearts and men will hold to it more firmly through adversity and discouragement than they would had their previous adherence been only nominal. This is what Milton meant when he wrote:

I cannot praise a fugitive and cloistered virtue, unexercised and unbreathed, that never sallies out and sees her adversary but slinks out of the race, when that immortal garland is to be run for and that not without dust and heat. . . . And though all the winds of doctrine were let loose to play upon the earth, so Truth be in the field, we do injuriously by licensing and prohibiting to misdoubt her strength. Let her and falsehood grapple; who ever knew Truth put to the worse, in a free and open encounter?

It was in this same spirit that Jefferson spoke, from this very building I believe, when on assuming the presidency in 1801, in that great reconciling first inaugural, he said of his extreme Federalist opponents, who had maligned him and many of whom wanted to dissolve the republic and set up a monarchy:

If there be any among us who would wish to dissolve this Union or to change its republican form, let them stand undisturbed as monuments of the safety with which error of opinion may be tolerated where reason is left free to combat it.

Fourth. But there is yet a stronger reason for tolerance and freedom of discussion. It is the basic argument for democracy itself, namely, that it makes people better. The moral life is one of choices. The man who never has to make decisions is neither interesting nor truly moral. It is the supreme merit of democracy that by making men and women voters and participants in public affairs it forces them to consider public issues, to make up their minds about them, and, finally, to choose. These very acts make them better men and women with broader interests than they would otherwise have in a police state where the decisions would be made by the few on top with the functions of the many limited only to those outlined in the slogan of Mussolini, "To believe, to obey, and to fight."

Thus opening the range of rational choice improves people and develops their qualities of reason and spiritual understanding. Narrowing that range by suppression deprives people of the chance for development. Characters like ideas are sharpened and toughened by conflict and choice. And true liberty provides just such opportunities which suppression takes away.

EQUALITY IN SACRIFICE [9]

PHILIP MURRAY [10]

Philip Murray, President of the Congress of Industrial Organizations, gave this speech on Wednesday, October 25, 1950, at the fourth session of the Nineteenth Annual Forum, conducted during October 23, 24 and 25, in the Grand Ballroom of the Waldorf-Astoria Hotel, New York City, under the auspices of the New York *Herald-Tribune*.

The panel addresses of this session under the chairmanship of W. Stuart Symington, then chairman of the National Security Resources Board, were on the topic "Mobilization in Action." Other members of the panel were Albert Goss, master of the National Grange, Mrs. Anna Rosenberg, then member of the United States National Commission for UNESCO, and Charles A. Patman, president of the National Association of Manufacturers.

President Murray's remarks (he also represented William Green, of the American Federation of Labor, and Albert Hayes, head of the International Association of Machinists) were in his usual direct vein— well organized and, on this occasion, highly condensed. They were significant, as outlining the philosophy that led in March 1951, to the revolt of organized labor, under the United Labor Policy Committee, against the Defense Mobilization Program.

We of the CIO are convinced that the American people have the skills and technique to mobilize quickly and effectively for the national emergency. Furthermore, the millions of men and women who make up our CIO organization have clearly indicated that they want the mobilization process to move with all possible speed.

Industrial workers—and their free labor unions—are a prime target for every dictatorship. The Nazis destroyed the German unions. The Communists, where they have achieved power, have subverted and corrupted the labor unions into instruments of the totalitarian state.

[9] Permission for reprinting was given through the courtesy of Mr. Philip Murray and of the New York *Herald Tribune*. For full proceedings of the Forum, see Section 10, New York *Herald Tribune* for October 29, 1950, "Annual Forum on Current Problems."

[10] For biographical note, see Appendix.

Fortunately for the American people, our labor organizations are strong, they are democratic and they are completely devoted to the welfare of our nation. Our unions are—they must be—a basic factor in the development of a healthy economy and a fully prepared defense establishment. A free society, such as we enjoy in the United States, cannot afford to ignore the hopes and aspirations and ideas of its working men and women.

The program of the CIO in this present emergency coincides with that of every decent, patriotic American citizen. We want speedy victory over the Communist aggressors in Korea—an event which happily seems close at hand.

We want our nation to build its military strength to a point where the Kremlin will realize that America has the power to stop aggression anywhere. This calls for definite goals, both military and civilian. Our government must forthrightly state its requirements now and for the foreseeable future.

Within the limits of necessary security, the American people are entitled to know all of the pertinent facts. This means a perspective of our productive requirements. This means a frank statement as to how many planes, how many tanks, how much of a military force we will need. This also means an equally frank statement as to how much steel, copper, aluminum, electric power and other resources must be produced to meet necessary military and civilian needs.

The guiding consideration must be the profound conviction, which we in the CIO share, that it is better to have too much in this emergency than too little.

A mobilization program that will help us achieve those goals must be based fairly and squarely upon the principle of "equality of sacrifice." Our mobilization program will lose the moral support of the people if it is perverted into a scheme to depress the living standards of the lower income groups—while the rich become even richer.

In my opinion, equality of sacrifice is indispensable to mobilizing our national resources for the tasks we face. Equality of sacrifice among all groups in the American public can be achieved. We can control inflation by appropriate means. We can take super-profits out of the defense effort, through vitally needed excess-profits taxes. We can make effective use of our manpower —without discrimination or bias because of race, creed, color, national origin or sex. We can overcome hysteria and work with clear heads to preserve our fundamental civil liberties.

And—by no means least—we can, and must, maintain an adequate wage level. This will help to improve the morale and productivity of the American industrial worker.

This is a reasonable program—a program to guarantee an effective basis for the mobilization process into which we are entering. It will give security and peace of mind to our citizens as they work and fight for security and peace throughout the world.

Nevertheless, there are persons and organizations in America who oppose a reasonable program of this kind. I do not know whether they act out of ignorance or out of a malicious spirit— the result is much the same. These apostles of reaction and fear would shift the burden of our national mobilization effort on to the workers. They propose special privileges for special business interests. They would give no heed to the problems and ideas of our working population. But I venture the thought that, in the final analysis, our security rests on the high morale of all the people.

Organized labor wants no monopoly of position or ideas in the mobilization program. Nor does the CIO believe that any one group—business men or farmers or professional people— should control our emergency planning.

Each group has much to offer, and much to learn. Together, we can build a team that will defeat anything the opposition has to offer. And the unions of America are ready to play their part.

HIGH COST OF BIGOTRY [11]

ERIC A. JOHNSTON [12]

Mr. Eric A. Johnston, Administrator of the Economic Stabilization Agency, gave this radio-television address on February 18, 1951, over the facilities of the American Broadcasting Company. As general chairman of Brotherhood Week, he spoke in connection with that program of February 18-24.

Mr. Johnston had frequently spoken on the necessity of tolerance and had a reputation for working vigorously against "propaganda against foreigners, Jews, Catholics, Negroes, and unionists."

His appointment in 1951 as a key figure in Economic Stabilization and his efforts to conciliate the interests of labor and management gave special significance to his remarks on brotherhood.

The oral style, characteristic of Johnston, is informal, highly concrete, and persuasive. He is an energetic, at times very rapid, speaker.[13]

I'd like to tell you now what I mean by brotherhood—and the best way to say it is to tell you what I don't mean by brotherhood.

My belief in brotherhood doesn't compel me to hold open house in my home around the clock, or go to lunch with somebody I don't like. Or go out of my way to be chummy with someone from a different church or with a different kind of ancestry.

My right to privacy and my right to select my friends are not amended one bit by feeling strongly on the subject of the brotherhood of man. I don't even have to say I'm tolerant to believe in brotherhood. And I don't have to be tolerant. In fact, I don't want to have to tolerate anybody. It's awfully uncomfortable to be in society of somebody that you think you have to tolerate.

Maybe I could put it this way: I don't want to be at the same table in a public place or anywhere else with a fellow who makes a heel out of himself.

[11] Text supplied and this reprint made possible through the courtesy of Eric A. Johnston.

[12] For biographical note, see Appendix.

[13] For further comment on Eric Johnston as a speaker, see *Representative American Speeches: 1944-45*, p175-6.

But I don't like the idea of kicking a man out of any door because he doesn't fit the Ku Klux Klan conception of a hundred per cent American.

My point is that I don't like bores, barflies, moochers, the bad mannered or the foul tongued, whether they are white or black; whether they belong to the church of Rome or the Sons and Daughters of I Will Arise. Or the church I go to myself.

Brotherhood, to me, doesn't mean showing off your tolerance. I think that's sappy, and it's insincere. Nobody is fooled for very long.

Brotherhood to me means behaving by the simple rules of decency to every decent person, regardless of how he parts his hair, the color of his skin, or the religious faith he follows.

Brotherhood means appraising the other fellow for what he's worth inside—as an associate in business—or as a social friend. Maybe the Elsie Dinsmores and the Little Lord Fauntleroys of this world can honestly say they love people in the mass. I can't. I've got to love them as people—as individuals.

And when you boil that down, what does it mean—except living by the American code that says the individual counts ahead of everything else? Let's explore that a little farther.

Now it seems to me that the blame for bigotry in this country is very largely heaped on the head of the native-born, white Protestant. If he'd only be nice and tolerant, why, we'd all get along as cozily as so many sleepy kittens in a basket. The way we get the story, that's the way it seems to go.

It just happened that I am native born, white and Protestant. My ancestors were the life of the party on some of the first ships to drop anchor off America; and if you take me somewhat farther back, the Johnstons of Scotland knew a little bit more about clans than those who spell the word with "K" in this country.

The Ku Klux Klanners would never take me in, of course, because I have the old-fashioned idea that bedsheets belong on the bedstead instead of over my head on horseback.

But as a native born, white Protestant, I sometimes think I'm discriminated against—and I am, when native born, white Protestants are singled as the sole perpetrators of intolerance. The fact is that individuals in every race among us, every faith among us, every ancestry among us are guilty of not abiding by the rules of brotherhood.

So it adds up that I take the rap when some other Americans of the same stock and faith as myself run amuck on the idea that America belongs to us and to us alone. I have to take a beating for their foolishness—in precisely the same way that the so-called minorities have to take the rap for the foolish sins of their own people.

Some of our hundred per cent Americans by self election who think they have a monopoly on the country have their precise counterparts in racial and religious blocs or lesser numerical strength. They must think they have a monopoly on the country too, for they organize politically to control it if they can. On that score, we are all sinners alike.

One of the grandest things about America is its human panorama—resulting from the intermingling of so many different peoples from so many different cultures. I hope the day will never come when Holland, Michigan, discards its tulip festival and throws away its title to a little piece of Holland in the heartland of America. I hope the day will never come when we cease to celebrate St. Patrick's day and jig to Irish tunes on the 17th of March. I want to see the rich folklore of other lands live on in America—but only aesthetically—not politically.

One of the saddest things about America is our hyphenated voting. So many times we go to the polls as Methodist-Americans, as Polish-Americans, as Catholic-Americans, as Jewish-Americans—as almost anything but what we ought to be—as all-Americans.

What kind of thinking is it that rallies votes against a candidate because his name ends in "ski," for instance, and rallies votes for a man because his name ends in "stein?"

It's not American thinking. That's for sure. It's not brotherhood. It's not decency. It's not common sense. It's plain damned foolishness—an expensive mistake of history.

The accident of birth gave me no right to think of myself as deserving something special from my country, but neither did the accident of birth give anybody else that right.

Truculence and belligerence and blanket name-calling won't get the so-called majority in this country anywhere in the long run—or the so-called minorities either. But every group of us that thinks of itself as a group has a chance to shame all the rest of us into sportsmanship by the exercise of sportsmanship itself.

The armor of courtesy is almost impossible to dent. But bigotry never built a bank balance, bought a bond, or gave a boost to the national income. Withholding jobs and business opportunities from one group doesn't make more jobs and more business opportunities for others. It simply serves as a drag on the whole economic engine. In ordinary times, you can't sell radios and refrigerators and automobiles to people who are denied decent jobs through bigotry.

We're in a showdown now. Look at the map. The Communist empire of Soviet Russia has scooped about 800 million into its sway. The Western world claims the allegiance of another 800 million. That leaves roughly 800 million—give or take a million either way—who could teeter toward the West—or totter toward the Kremlin.

They are mostly all in Asia. And while they may have large misgivings about communism, I haven't noticed any wild enthusiasms among them for the West—either before America came into the Western leadership—or since.

We talk about building bridges of brotherhood around the world in answer to the Communist pretensions. And communism, as we all know, makes a great deal of phony fuss and feathers about the brotherhood of man.

But where does brotherhood begin? It begins on a man-to-man basis here at home and not on a mass-to-mass basis across the oceans. Without that footing, a bridge of brotherhood is idle talk and empty vision. And ours is just as phony in the eyes of Asia as the Communists'.

Ahead of us all is the job of trying to make our democracy work better than it ever has, for it's got to if it's going to last; ahead of us is the job of proving to ourselves and to the world that the greatest experiment of all time—the American system—

works for the good of all Americans: that it has justified the faith and hope of all mankind.

That's the kind of society men have been groping for through all the ages. It is here, if we want it to be here—the great and good beginning of a universal brotherhood of men.

POLITICAL SCENE

VOTE REPUBLICAN [1]

ROBERT A. TAFT [2]

Senator Robert Taft, just concluding his prolonged Ohio campaign for reelection in 1950, replied on Sunday, November 5, to President Truman's St. Louis address of the previous night. The reply was broadcast over a special Ohio network from Cincinnati and was limited to fifteen minutes.

His talk is a highly condensed version of arguments on which he had previously spent many hours in the United States Senate and in the Ohio state campaign. The campaign itself he had initiated a year before. He had spoken in every county—and in some, several times. Money poured in for his campaign from nearly all parts of the country. His opponent, Joseph T. Ferguson, was strongly supported by all labor organizations. The campaign attracted nation-wide attention.

He made the issue one of inflation and the high costs of government and taxes, "passed on to the poor old consumer." He combatted the Truman assumption that the social security and the 75-cent minimum wage were due to the Democratic party. His logic was to examine the *causes,* favorable and unfavorable, that resulted in present legislation and governmental programs, and to attach the proper agency for those causes. He thus assailed the logic by which Truman attacked and blamed the Republicans.

Taft's speech of reply is distinctive in its effort to show that Truman resorted to "special pleading" by ignoring important issues and important facts related to recent governmental history. The full listing of topics and facts ignored by Truman made the Taft rebuttal a powerful document.

Because the speech was so short, Taft presumably omitted the many persuasive elements that might have given more vividness to his logic. Rhetorical questions would have sharpened the issues and more graphic language might have given the short refutation more popular appeal. The Ohio voters, however, familiar with the Taft techniques of public speech and debate and with his oft-repeated onslaughts against his opponents, needed for their conviction only this straight Republican indictment of Truman.

[1] Text furnished through the courtesy of the Taft-for-Senate Committee, Cincinnati, Ohio.

[2] For biographical note, see Appendix.

Taft's victory on November 7 was complete. In the campaign of 1938 he had won by 170,000; in 1944, by 17,999; in 1950, by a plurality of 430,879, out of the total vote of 2,698,000. His popular vote was 1,642,537. He carried all but four of eighty-eight counties, and every large industrial district. In view of the campaign against him by the combined forces of the CIO and the AFL United Mine Workers, his victory was all the more significant. Frank J. Lausche, Democrat, was elected Governor by a plurality of 146,152. Taft thus emerged as a stronger candidate than ever, and as a possible Republican nominee for the presidency in 1952.[8]

Last night President Truman appealed to the people to vote for Democratic candidates for Congress in order to give him complete control of Congress for the enactment of any program —domestic or foreign—he might submit. Of course, we have a Democratic Congress today, but it has rejected or neglected most of Mr. Truman's policies—economic controls, government entry into business, the Brannan Plan, socialized medicine and repeal of the Taft-Hartley Law, altogether making up the Socialist program demanded by the Political Action Committee of the CIO and recommended repeatedly to Congress by Mr. Truman himself. Such a program, of course, would have imposed on the people of this country a complete direction of their lives by Washington bureaus, detailed regulation of commerce, industry and agriculture, of all business and all farms, federal handouts to all, and federal regulation of all health and welfare services in the United States, now the concern and the pride of thousands of charitable institutions and of local communities.

Evidently Mr. Truman realizes that the Brannan Plan and socialized medicine and economic controls are against every instinct of the American voter and in fact have almost been dropped by some Democratic candidates. And so when he sums up his program at the end of his speech, he doesn't use the names of these proposals so the people may understand what he is talking about. He reduces the Brannan Plan to a "system of marketing farm products that will stabilize income," and he speaks of socialized medicine as "a workable health insurance

---

[8] For comment on Taft as speaker and for other examples of his addresses, see *Representative American Speeches: 1938-1939*, p119-37; *1945-1946*, p154-63; *1946-1947*, p196-202; *1947-1948*, p103-17.

system to help people pay their doctors' bills," but, of course, they are the same old plans and he has recommended every item of his control program to Congress three times. He is committed to the Political Action Committee if he and they can once get control of a rubber-stamp Congress.

Of course, there is the usual claptrap in the speech prepared for the President about the Hoover depression and the 80th Congress and isolationism. Of course, it is true that a national depression started when the Republicans were in power. It is also true that the first World War started when the Democrats were in power. It is also true that the Second World War started when the Democrats were in power, that the Korean War has occurred under Mr. Truman himself. It is also true that the death of 300,000 American boys in World War II is certainly as much to be regretted as the hard times of the 30's. One argument is about as good as the other.

As usual, Mr. Truman claims credit for bringing the people back from the depression of 1932. Surely, the people's memory may be short, but surely they can remember that after seven years of the Roosevelt Administration, after seven years of New Deal measures and all sorts of proposals which promised to bring the millenium, we still had 10 million people unemployed in 1939, and a farm income of about half of what it ought to be. It was war and war alone that brought back prosperity, and there is certainly a false note in prosperity based on a public debt of $256 billion and continuous deficits and huge government expenditures for arms.

The President's speech is more notable for what he does not say than for what he does say. He doesn't mention the high prices which every housewife has to pay today. He boasts of all the things he is giving the workmen, but he doesn't say anything about the prices or taxes that they pay in prices. The people can't hope for any increase in their standard of living on this kind of program. Every increase in wages is balanced by higher prices and higher taxes. It is all done with mirrors—something for nothing to everybody. Parity prices to the farmer, unlimited loans to all, free medicine, unlimited power to labor to obtain any wage they desire, free gifts to the entire world. Even the taxpayer can't stand it in the end. It can only be done by printing money and killing the value of the dollar. Prices have gone up because the administration for political purposes, wanted prosperity at least until November 7. As usual, they are running a huge deficit. They only balanced the budget when they had a Republican Congress, but this year they not only have a deficit, but they have encouraged the increase of bank loans, credit of all kinds and brought about deliberately the increase in prices and the inflation which we now face by putting $16 billion of inflationary money into the economy between July 1, 1949 and July 1, 1950.

Already our government is spending more money than we have ever spent in peacetime and yet the President wants the Brannan Plan which might cost $5 billion, socialized medicine that will cost another $6 billion and his program has made huge spending necessary for the armed forces. In fact, your own freedom has been limited by this huge taxation. Just add up the money deducted from your pay over the year, and then remember besides that when you buy food or clothing or shoes or anything else, the price includes about 20 per cent of taxes paid along the way by the farmer, the railroad, the manufacturer, the retailer and all the rest of them. Altogether the government takes more than 25 per cent of the national income in taxes. You work one day in four for the government, and only three for yourself. Most of those taxes are passed on to the poor old consumer.

The President doesn't mention civil rights or the program which he promised and promised and wholly failed to enact in the present Democratic Congress. The truth is that under this Congress a majority of the Democrats voted against shutting down the filibuster which prevents the enactment of such a program. Twenty-six Democrats voted against such a procedure, nineteen only voted to close the filibuster. The truth is that no civil rights program ever will be enacted as long as we have a Democratic Congress with a powerful position occupied therein by the Southern Democrats.

In order to make the President's case against the 80th Congress, he had wholly to misrepresent the facts as to what they did. He says for instance that they took social security from a million people. They didn't take social security away from anybody who had it, and they prepared the bill which was finally enacted this year with bi-partisan approval adding 10 million people to the social security rolls and increasing the benefits by 77 per cent. That bill went through this Congress because my Republican colleagues and I backed it, and as a matter of fact I think I was as active and responsible for it as any Senator, Democrat or Republican, in the Senate.

The same thing goes for the 75-cent minimum wage for which the President claims credit. The President says that the 80th Congress passed a rich man's tax bill. The fact is that they took seven million people of the lower income taxpayers entirely off the rolls and they reduced everybody's taxes. Now the President's 81st Congress has just increased all those taxes again. The President says nothing of the huge taxes which he is going to recommend to be passed by the next Congress. The President says the 80th Congress attacked the farmers' price support program. The truth is that they enacted the Aiken price support bill, the most scientific price support bill that has ever been worked out, backed by the American Farm Bureau Federation and by the National Grange and signed with approval by Mr. Truman himself. Surely, his memory is short!

He says the 80th Congress started to destroy labor because they passed the Taft-Hartley Law. Why, after three years of that law the American workman is better off than he ever has been before. Only the arbitrary powers of the labor boss have been curtailed. Recent polls show an increase of 50 per cent during the past year in the number of union members who approve the Taft-Hartley Law because it protects them against the arbitrary action of labor union bosses as well as against the arbitrary action of arbitrary employers.

He accused his opponents, of course, of being isolationists and subject to special interests, but he said not a word about greed and privilege in his home bailiwick of Kansas City or in the Missouri where he himself spoke, or in the White House itself. Mr. Truman himself spoke in behalf of Mr. Tom Pendergast on the Senate floor after Mr. Pendergast's conviction in a Federal court, as Senator Ferguson pointed out. Senator Ferguson inquired regarding the privilege represented by Mayor Curley of Boston, pardoned by the President for mail frauds, of those four members of the Capone gang paroled from the penitentiary, or Mr. John Maragon, friend of General Harry Vaughn. What about the vote frauds and ballot-stealing cases in Kansas City quietly passed over by the Department of Justice? What kind of special interests are represented by those people who have received favors from the administration?

But the President's greatest omission relates to the war. Anybody who disagrees with his foreign policy is an isolationist. He says nothing of the fact that it was his administration which built up Russia to the point where it indeed today is a threat to the security of our people. He says nothing of the Yalta agreements, which he approved at Potsdam, which gave Berlin and Prague and Vienna to Russia when our boys could have taken both Berlin and Prague. They were on their way to Berlin long before the Russians got there and they were called back because of the agreements made at Yalta. General Patton was in Czechoslovakia, would have taken Prague the next day when he was stopped because, under the agreement made at Yalta, it was understood that the Czechs should surrender to the Russians. He says nothing of the Alger Hiss influence at Yalta which led Harry Hopkins and Averell Harriman and himself to speak of Russia as a peace-loving democracy. That certainly is a complete delusion, probably the most dangerous delusion which any of our policymakers have ever embraced.

He says nothing of the building up of the Chinese Communists by this administration. Remember they put Russia in full control in Manchuria contrary to every principle of American foreign policy in the Far East since the days of John Hay and without even telling the Nationalist government for four months that they had bargained away the most important industrial province of China. He says nothing of the fact that this Chinese-Communist power, which is slaughtering American boys in Korea today, was encouraged by his administration. He tried to force Chiang Kai-shek to take these Communists into his cabinet. He refused him military aid when he would not comply. He says nothing of the fact that Secretary Acheson wanted to recognize the Chinese Communists, that he sent out word to the State Department representatives that the American people must be conditioned for the taking over of Formosa by the Chinese Communists. He says nothing of the fact that the Korean attack was encouraged by Secretary Acheson's formal pronouncement that we would never defend Formosa or any other point beyond Japan, Okinawa and the Philippines. There certainly was nothing isolationist about my demand that we defend Formosa and stop the advance of communism wherever it is feasible to do so. It was his administration which pursued the isolationist policy which brought on the Korean War and built up Chinese Communists to a position where today we face a major war seven thousand miles from home.

As for sabotaging the bipartisan foreign policy Mr. Truman himself killed that policy from the date of his election in November of 1948.

Mr. Truman avoids entirely the sacrifices which his policy would impose upon the American people. He doesn't want to mention those before November 7. They may well require the drafting of every American boy of nineteen for two years' service in the army. They will certainly involve taxes higher than we have ever levied on our people before. These sacrifices result directly from the fact that this administration has lost the peace after the American people won the war.

POLITICAL CONSCIENCE [4]

MARGARET CHASE SMITH [5]

Senator Margaret Chase Smith gave this speech before the United States Senate on June 1, 1950. At the conclusion she read the "Declaration of Conscience" drafted by her and subscribed to by six other Republican Senators.

Her speech was highly personal, free from the usual political platitudes. She was dramatic in her compositional methods and content. The conclusion to the declaration furnished a stirring and unexpected climax to her remarks, and the added signatures gave prestige to her discourse.

The castigation of the Republicans was widely interpreted as applying chiefly to Senator Joseph McCarthy. The Wisconsin Senator, since his speech of February 9, 1950, had been busy attempting to expose communism in high governmental places. Before the Senate Foreign Relations Committee, for example, he had charged that the State Department was "infested" with pro-Communists. He had attacked Owen Lattimore as Russia's "top espionage agent in America." Senator McCarthy named various others as pro-Communists. On the floor of the Senate he had denounced Lattimore and others who had been associated with the State Department.

At the conclusion of her speech Senator H. Alexander Smith, Republican of New Jersey said, "I wish to state that I am in wholehearted agreement with everything she has said, and I congratulate her and commend her for the magnificent address she has just made to the Senate."

Senator Smith, a native of Skowhegan, Maine, had been a school teacher, a member of the staff of the *Independent-Reporter* of Skowhegan, had worked in a woolen mill, and after the death of her husband, Congressman Smith, in 1940, had been elected as Congresswoman from Maine for four terms. Without machine support in Maine she entered the 1948 Senate race, and in the Maine primaries she carried fourteen of the sixteen counties with more ballots than her three male opponents combined. She campaigned with unbounded energy throughout the state and with much public speaking effectiveness. She established a reputation as a liberal and since becoming a Senator she continued her independent position.

Her speech of June 1 was significant as an expression of dissatisfaction with the conservative wing of Republicanism. The progressive

---

[4] Text furnished by Senator Margaret Chase Smith. See also *Congressional Record* 96:8000-8002, June 1, 1950 (daily edition).

[5] For biographical note, see Appendix.

block which she represented was small but potent. Those who signed the Margaret Smith declaration were comparative newcomers in the Senate, but were nevertheless outspoken and were critical of the Taft-Hoover-Wherry group. Four of the Senators who signed the document (Smith, Tobey, Aiken, and Morse) were up for reelection in the November election. All were reelected, Tobey and Morse after hard fights.

Mr. President: I would like to speak briefly and simply about a serious national condition. It is a national feeling of fear and frustration that could result in national suicide and the end of everything that we Americans hold dear. It is a condition that comes from the lack of effective leadership in either the legislative branch or the executive branch of our government. That leadership is so lacking that serious and responsible proposals are being made that national advisory commissions be appointed to provide such critically needed leadership.

I speak as briefly as possible because too much harm has already been done with irresponsible words of bitterness and selfish political opportunism. I speak as simply as possible because the issue is too great to be obscured by eloquence. I speak simply and briefly in the hope that my words will be taken to heart. I speak as a Republican. I speak as a woman. I speak as a United States Senator. I speak as an American.

The United States Senate has long enjoyed world-wide respect as the greatest deliberative body in the world. But recently that deliberative character has too often been debased to the level of a forum of hate and character assassination sheltered by the shield of congressional immunity.

It is ironical that we Senators can in debate in the Senate directly or indirectly, by any form of words impute to any American, who is not a senator, any conduct or motive unworthy or unbecoming an American—and without that non-senator American having any legal redress against us—yet if we say the same thing in the Senate about our colleagues we can be stopped on the grounds of being out of order.

It is strange that we can verbally attack anyone else without restraint and with full protection and yet we hold ourselves above the same type of criticism here on the Senate floor. Surely the United States Senate is big enough to take self-criticism and self-appraisal. Surely we should be able to take the same kind of character attacks that we "dish out" to outsiders.

I think that it is high time for the United States Senate and its members to do some soul searching—for us to weigh our consciences—on the manner in which we are performing our duty to the people of America—on the manner in which we are using or abusing our individual powers and privileges.

I think that it is high time that we remembered that we have sworn to uphold and defend the Constitution. I think that it is high time that we remembered that the Consitution, as amended, speaks not only of the freedom of speech but also of trial by jury instead of trial by accusation. Whether it be a criminal prosecution in court or a character prosecution in the Senate, there is little practical distinction when the life of a person has been ruined.

Those of us who shout loudest about Americanism in making character assassinations are all too frequently those who, by our own words and acts, ignore some of the basic principles of Americanism—the right to criticize; the right to hold unpopular beliefs; the right to protest; the right of independent thought.

The exercise of these rights should not cost one single American citizen his reputation or his right to a livelihood, nor should he be in danger of losing his reputation or livelihood merely because he happens to know some one who holds unpopular beliefs. Who of us doesn't? Otherwise none of us could call our souls our own. Otherwise thought control would have set in.

The American people are sick and tired of being afraid to speak their minds lest they be politically smeared as "Communists" or "Fascists" by their opponents. Freedom of speech is not what it used to be in America. It has been so abused by some that it is not exercised by others. The American people are sick and tired of seeing innocent people smeared and guilty people whitewashed. But there have been enough proved cases to cause nation-wide distrust and strong suspicion that there may be something to the unproved, sensational accusations.

As a Republican, I say to my colleagues on this side of the aisle that the Republican Party faces a challenge today that is not unlike the challenge that it faced back in Lincoln's day. The Republican Party so successfully met that challenge that it emerged from the Civil War—as the champion of a united nation—in addition to being a party that unrelentingly fought loose spending and loose programs.

Today our country is being psychologically divided by the confusion and the suspicions that are bred in the United States Senate to spread like cancerous tenacles of "know nothing, suspect everything" attitudes. Today we have a Democratic Administration that has developed a mania for loose spending and loose programs. History is repeating itself—and the Republican Party again has the opportunity to emerge as the champion of unity and prudence.

The record of the present Democratic Administration has provided us with sufficient campaign issues without the necessity of resorting to political smears. America is rapidly losing its position as leader of the world simply because the Democratic Administration has pitifully failed to provide effective leadership.

The Democratic Administration has completely confused the American people by its daily contradictory grave warnings and optimistic assurances—that show the people that our Democratic Administration has no idea of where it is going. The Democratic Administration has greatly lost the confidence of the American people by its complacency to the threat of communism here at home and the leak of vital secrets to Russia through key officials of the Democratic Administration. There are enough proved cases to make this point without diluting our criticism with unproved charges.

Surely these are sufficient reasons to make it clear to the American people that it is time for a change and that a Republican victory is necessary to the security of this country. Surely it is clear that this nation will continue to suffer as long as it is governed by the present ineffective Democratic Administration.

Yet to displace it with a Republican regime embracing a philosophy that lacks political integrity or intellectual honesty would prove equally disastrous to this nation. The nation sorely needs a Republican victory. But I don't want to see the Republican Party ride to political victory on the Four Horsemen of Calumny—Fear, Ignorance, Bigotry and Smear. I doubt if the Republican Party could—simply because I don't believe the American people will uphold any political party that puts political exploitation above national interest. Surely we Republicans aren't that desperate for victory.

I don't want to see the Republican Party win that way. While it might be a fleeting victory for the Republican Party, it would be a more lasting defeat for the American people. Surely it would ultimately be suicide for the Republican Party and the two-party system that has protected our American liberties from the dictatorship of a one-party system.

As members of the minority party, we do not have the primary authority to formulate the policy of our government. But we do have the responsibility of rendering constructive criticism, of clarifying issues, of allaying fears by acting as responsible citizens.

As a woman, I wonder how the mothers, wives, sisters and daughters feel about the way in which members of their families have been politically mangled in Senate debate—and I use the word "debate" advisedly.

As a United States Senator, I am not proud of the way in which the Senate has been made a publicity platform for irresponsible sensationalism. I am not proud of the reckless abandon in which unproved charges have been hurled from this side of the aisle. I am not proud of the obviously staged, undignified countercharges that have been attempted in retaliation from the other side of the aisle.

I don't like the way the Senate has been made a rendezvous for vilification, for selfish political gain at the sacrifice of individual reputations and national unity. I am not proud of the way we smear outsiders from the floor of the Senate and hide behind the cloak of congressional immunity and still place ourselves beyond criticism on the floor of the Senate.

As an American, I am shocked at the way Republicans and Democrats alike are playing directly into the Communist design of "confuse, divide and conquer." As an American, I don't want a Democratic Administration "whitewash" or "cover up" any more than I want a Republican smear or witch hunt.

As an American, I condemn a Republican "Fascist" just as much as I condemn a Democrat "Communist." I condemn a Democrat "Fascist" just as much as I condemn a Republican "Communist." They are equally dangerous to you and me and to our country. As an American, I want to see our nation recapture the strength and unity it once had when we fought the enemy instead of ourselves.

It is with these thoughts that I have drafted what I call a "Declaration of Conscience." I am gratified that Senator Tobey, Senator Aiken, Senator Morse, Senator Ives, Senator Thye and Senator Hendrickson, have concurred in that declaration and have authorized me to announce their concurrence.

Statement of Seven Republican Senators

1. We are Republicans. But we are Americans first. It is as Americans we express our concern with the growing confusion that threatens the security and stability of our country. Democrats and Republicans alike have contributed to that confusion.

2. The Democratic Administration has initially created the confusion by its lack of effective leadership, by its contradictory grave warnings and optimistic assurances, by its complacency to the threat of communism here at home, by its oversensitiveness to rightful criticism, by its petty bitterness against its critics.

3. Certain elements of the Republican Party have materially added to this confusion in the hopes of riding the Republican Party to victory through the selfish political exploitation of fear, bigotry, ignorance and intolerance. There are enough mistakes of the Democrats for Republicans to criticize constructively without resorting to political smears.

4. To this extent, Democrats and Republicans alike have unwittingly, but undeniably, played directly into the Communist design of "confuse, divide and conquer."

5. It is high time that we stopped thinking politically as Republicans and Democrats about elections and started thinking patriotically as Americans about national security based on individual freedom. It is high time that we all stopped being tools

and victims of totalitarian techniques—techniques that, if continued here unchecked, will surely end what we have come to cherish as the American way of life.

Margaret Chase Smith, Maine

Charles W. Tobey, New Hampshire

George D. Aiken, Vermont

Wayne L. Morse, Oregon

Irving M. Ives, New York

Edward J. Thye, Minnesota

Robert C. Hendrickson, New Jersey

EDUCATION

THE ACT OF FAITH [1]

ARCHIBALD MACLEISH [2]

Archibald MacLeish, Boylston Professor of Rhetoric and Oratory at Harvard since 1949, gave this address at the inauguration of Margaret Clapp as President of Wellesley College, at Alumni Hall Auditorium, Wellesley, Massachusetts, on March 17, 1950.

MacLeish's address made a profound impression on his academic audience. The speaker's delivery although restrained was emphatic and persuasive. His considerable pitch range and excellent voice quality were assets to his presentation.

The address had distinctive rhetorical virtues. The thinking was original, stimulating, constructive, based upon an analysis of the national and international events of the hour. The discourse had structural design and movement; adaptation to the audience; unconventionality of expression; oral quality; genuine eloquence. The ideas, purpose, and mode of expression were characteristic of MacLeish—the product of his experience and development as writer and speaker.[3]

Except for Banquo's ghost, who is present but is not expected to talk, I can think of no role less relevant to its occasion than that of the speaker at the inauguration of the president of an institution of learning.

It is not his place to welcome the new president to her post: the young ladies have seen to that.

It is not his function to compliment the trustees on their good taste and sound judgment in her selection: the trustees have never questioned their possession of either quality, and besides they have the proof before them.

[1] Text is from the *Wellesley College News*, March 30, 1950. The address was also published in *The Atlantic Monthly* 185:31-4, June 1950. This reprinting is through the courtesy of Dr. Archibald MacLeish and with permission of the Atlantic Monthly Company.

[2] For biographical note, see Appendix.

[3] For further comment on Archibald MacLeish, see *Representative American Speeches: 1941-1942*, p75-90; *1943-1944*, p243-7; *1944-1945*, p186-9.

It is not his privilege to remind the new incumbent of the superlative merits of her predecessor, of which she is only too anxiously aware, or to reassure her as to her own abundant qualifications to succeed that famous lady: everyone within sight of the platform is already and entirely satisfied on both points.

It is not even his duty to advise the new administration on the educational policy it should pursue—though I would not go so far as to contend that he never offers his willing back to that enticing burden.

His sole function—if it can be called a function—is to expose to an audience concerned, and properly concerned, with something else, his private thoughts—which may or may not merit or survive exposure.

My private thoughts on this occasion can be compressed to one: a lively sense of the astonishing paradox of our presence in this room, for this purpose, in this year of the republic's history.

Here is a great and distinctly American college making the most emphatic affirmation of belief in the national future of which men are capable. And here, in the same country, and in the same hour, and from one end of the American republic to the other, is something as different from that affirmation, as opposite to it, as contradictory, as the human mind would well conceive: a fear for the future, a nightmare terror of the future, a total lack of confidence in the future such as the world has not seen since the decade of the millenium, if, indeed, it saw it then.

To educate at all is to profess a faith in the future of the most explicit kind, since education, by its nature, assumes the future. To make a new beginning in education—and in educational institutions a new administration is always a new beginning, for it is by this method that educational institutions, like other shell-forming animals, achieve their growth—to make a new beginning in education is to reaffirm that profession of faith and reassert it in a new confidence for the years ahead. Neither a new president, nor her officers, nor her trustees, nor her students could commit themselves to a new administration of the college unless they believed in the future—unless they believed .that there would be a future—unless they believed that there was still time.

And yet, if we may trust what we hear, and what we our-selves say, and what goes on echoing in our minds even in this room and even at this moment, the people of this country have no such confidence. If we may trust what we hear, and what we find ourselves saying, and what our newspapers and our poli-ticians tell us morning after morning, evening after evening, it is our conviction, both as a people and as a government, that we are already engaged in an ineluctable struggle for survival with force or the threat of force as its necessary means and those means expressed in weapons so implacably destructive that they may well wipe out all human life across an entire continent—not inconceivably our own.

So convinced are we of the inevitability of this threat or use of force that talk about the negotiation of peace is discouraged as wishful thinking by the Democratic Department of State on one side, and denounced as subversive activity by Republican politicians and newspapers on the other.

So certain are we of the impossibility of a peaceful settlement that a small group of Senators and Members of Congress, un-distinguished and unrespected men but raucously self-assured of their political sagacity, are busily preparing even now to make the next national election a competition in patrioteering with the prize of office to go to the man or the party which can prove that it has hated Russia loudest, longest and with the most irresponsible invective.

Confidence in peace, confidence in the future, the natural, normal, decent confidence of men of courage and character in their country and themselves, has all but vanished from the Congress of the United States. And in the prolonged and in-explicable silence of the President there are few voices raised anywhere for what we used to think of as the American cause: the cause of the human future.

These two things, the affirmation of belief in the future, the surrender to fear for the future, do not go together. Above all, they do not go together in this room. If you are educating young men and young women for life, to live their lives—which, as Miss Clapp says, is what liberal education is—you are not educating them for a vast and terrible struggle for survival to be fought between civilian populations, first with terror, and then with scientific devices for extermination.

And if, by the same sign, you believe that you are engaged in such a struggle of competitive terrorization and eventual destruction of civilian populations, with survival, to say nothing of "victory," depending on the reactions of your people to attack, you will not offer young men and young women liberal education. You will offer instead the kind of education some of our more demoralized politicians propose even now for the production of scientists. You will produce not men and women but coldwar soldiers, reared in antiseptic ignorance of every doubt or hope or aspiration, indoctrinated rather than instructed, whose neuter and unasking minds, packed with creed instead of questions like so many sawdust dolls, will give to every stimulus the appropriate response. It is not only the bigger bombs and the bigger bombers of the jingo press we need. If we are really engaged in a civilian struggle for survival our greatest need is for a civilian population disciplined for such a struggle. We need, not colleges and universities, but arsenals of human beings. And we need them now.

These two things, the act of confidence in the future here, the terror of the future everywhere and here as well, can simply not be reconciled. They cannot live together. And yet they do. They do, within this room. How do they?

Is it because people like us, people of our kind, live our lives in separate compartments?—because we don't permit ourselves to know, as officers and teachers and students and friends of this college, what we know only too well, what we lie awake at night knowing, as men and women?—because we go on with our lives and our occupations out of habit and out of sheer inertia, repeating, now that they are meaningless, the forms and motions that once had meaning when the future was alive?

Is it because we deceive ourselves with hopes which we know only too well are deceptions—the hope that something will turn up now, that something will happen, that Stalin will die or the Communists will change their minds or the Tito-ists will overthrow the Kremlin and everything will be different; the hope that the cold war can be won as a cold war, in spite of the fact that a cold war, by hypothesis, is a war that can never be won because it is waged, not to accomplish something, but to prevent something from happening, and is therefore only effective as long as it goes on preventing?

Is it because we delude ourselves into thinking that somehow, in some way, by some miracle, we will be spared in this holocaust—our lives will be spared, or our days, or our college or this particular new beginning we inaugurate this morning? Is it because we think, like the Princess in Li Po's poem, that the howling of the yellow dogs is not for us?

I, for myself, do not think so. I do not think it is for any of these reasons we are able to do what we are doing here today. I do not think we are deluding ourselves, or hiding our fears from our hopes, or carrying on out of habit, or pretending not to know what in fact we do know.

I think the truth is the opposite. I think the truth is that we do *not* know what we pretend to know—what we pretend to know because we hear ourselves saying it over and over like parrots, or because we read it over and over in the speech the hypnotized politicians are constantly making—the same speech over and over with nothing but the speaker changing.

I think we *do not know*—we here in this room and millions of others in millions of other rooms across this country—I think we *do not* know that our time is a time of ineluctable war, of inescapable struggle for survival, which weapons and warfare must decide because only weapons and warfare can decide it.

I think we do not know this because we know it is not true. And I think the reason we know it is not true is not that we are childish as a people but precisely that we are not childish. To believe that the great crises of human history are not resolved by threats and not resolved by arms is not childish. To believe that the fundamental choice between individual freedom and institutional authority which our world must make is not a choice which bombs can make for us, and therefore not a choice which bombs will make for us, is not childish. The childish thing is the infantile mentality, the movie-magazine mind, which thinks a crisis like the crisis of our age can be the work of a handful of conspiratorial Communists, and can be resolved and therefore must be resolved by weapons.

We know very well we must arm ourselves for our own defense in a world in which Russia is armed. But we do not know, because we do not believe, that arms will be enough no matter how many, no matter how powerful. We do not believe this, because we do not believe the decision can be reached by arms. We do not believe that what is in issue in our time is susceptible of armed decision.

There could be war. There could easily be war. Russian conduct over the past three years has been provocative and infuriating: a combination of calculated bluster and blundering deceit which only the gangster underworld could equal. The conduct of some Americans has been stupid and provocative also. It would be hard to equal, anywhere but in Russia itself, the irresponsibility and recklessness of certain members of the last two Congresses and certain newspapers and certain columnists. But because we could blunder into war with Russia through stupidity on either side, it does not follow that war with Russia is inevitable. And it is the inevitability of war which is the central question for this country because it is the shadow of that fatality which freezes the creative impulses of our lives and exposes the most precious thing in America—the independence and self-respect of individual citizens—to the campaigns of dishonor and defamation which have become the political stock in trade of ambitious and unprincipled politicians—who are not altogether nameless.

What is really in issue between the Russians and ourselves— what the evangelists of the inevitable conflict talk about day after day—is difference in belief. War is inevitable because our beliefs are different and because neither can live in a world dominated by the other. We, in the United States, must have a world in which individual liberty can thrive, for unless individual liberty can thrive throughout the world it cannot thrive here. The Russians must have a world in which authority is safe from freedom, for unless authority is safe from the aspirations of freedom everywhere it is safe from them nowhere. Therefore, the preachment goes, war must someday come and until it comes the threat of war must be maintained.

But the evangelists of war forget two things. And it is these two things we and people like us remember whatever words we use. They forget, first, that when they talk about the world they are not talking about the people of Russia and the United States alone. They are talking as well about 1400 million others who are now stirring and moving in the long dream of their history as men have never stirred and moved before. Whether the world will be authoritarian or free will depend on the 1400 million as well as on ourselves. It will depend on the world they make for themselves—the world they are even now in the process of making. For the great central fact before us, the fact to which the evangelists of war have shut their eyes, is the new world—the fact that a new and wholly different world is in the process of creation in our time.

That is one thing the evangelists of war forget. And the other is this: that creation is not accomplished with weapons. You cannot make a world with weapons. You cannot shape a world in the image of liberty with weapons. You cannot even shape a world in the image of authority with weapons. Arms can be used to put down freedom, as they have been used again and again in human history. Arms can be used to overthrow authority, as we used them once, and as other peoples have used them before and since. But they cannot be used to create. And the problem, both for us and for the Russians is to create—to create in the new world the kind of life we severally believe in, the one kind or the other. It is there, on that battlefield, on the competitive battlefield of creative labor, not on the impotent battlefield of exterminating war, that the real issue will be decided. It is that struggle which is inescapable; that conflict, and not the conflict of arms, which must be faced.

To which the realists reply: Ah, yes, but do the Russians know it? What will the Russians be doing while we create a world? Cutting our throats? Blasting us off the earth? No, there's nothing the Russians understand but force: nothing they respect but facts in being. All we can do is face them with force and facts until—what? The voice drags off into silence. Until they recognize the facts and say so? And what then? Will we believe what they say? Or go on with the force and the facts in the same old impotence until we come to the one conclusion to which force and facts invariably lead—the conclusion the hard-headed men have been telling us all along we would come to—the conclusion of war?

It is one of the defects of the American educational system, and has been for generations, that it turns out a self-styled "realist" mentality which equates belief in life with gullibility, and regards a fact as only a fact when it is ugly. No one can say of course what the Russians think. But every indication we have— even the sadistic and brutal trials and the palpably engineered "confessions"—every indication we have suggests that the Russians know very well where the struggle will be decided. Why otherwise torture their victims for confessions of guilt involving their enemies? Why not shoot them off-hand and be done with it? It is not for themselves or for us these grizzly dramas are played out but for the audience of the world.

When the Russians announced a little while ago that they were developing atomic energy for the purpose of peace—to "free mankind from its ancient servitude to toil," the hard-headed realists in America shouted "propaganda." What the Russians were really doing they said, was to build atomic bombs —hydrogen bombs maybe—anyway bombs. Perhaps it was propaganda: if it was, it was good propaganda for the 1400 million—better propaganda than ours with our promise of death by incineration on a bigger and better model than Hiroshima. But perhaps also—as a writer in the *Christian Science Monitor* quietly pointed out—perhaps it wasn't propaganda after all. Perhaps the Russians really knew what they were doing. Perhaps they realized that a great new source of industrial power put at the disposal of their political philosophy might give them an advantage, previously enjoyed by us, in the struggle for men's minds. Perhaps nothing would suit them better in Russia than precisely the delusive realism of our realistic men: the concentration upon bombs and weapons while the Russians went about their business of constructing the means to wage the actual struggle—the struggle for the creation of a world.

The *Monitor* correspondent may be right. But whatever the Russians intend or believe, the explanation of the American paradox lies in the fact that a great part of the American people feels in its bones, whatever words it may find in its mouth, that the conflict which divides our time is not a Russian-American conflict only, to be waged by facing up to the Soviets with a show of defensive force, however necessary the possession of a defensive force may be. A great part of the American people believes that the real conflict is a very different conflict, a much broader conflict—a conflict for the soul and spirit of a world now coming into being: a new world. It is this profound conviction which explains the national restlessness under the negative and defensive foreign policy of the past four years. It is this conviction which explains the failure of the Formosa Party in the Senate, even with the support of powerful sections of the press, to make any impression whatever on the country. It is this conviction which supported the enormous and spontaneous enthusiasm aroused by the McMahon proposals. It is this conviction which is expressed from day to day across the country in actions like the action in this room, actions directed toward the future in confidence and faith. There is a considerable body of Americans who, for all the talk, for all their talk, do not believe in the inevitable war, do not believe in the inescapable disaster, do not believe that the destiny of the Americans is to resist history and to oppose it, do not believe that the appearance of communism, or the rise of Russia, or the invention of atomic bombs, has changed the role this people has to play. There is a considerable body of Americans who believe that the great decisions of history are made not by death but by life, and that we have a stake in life, and a talent for life, and that it is there, in the shaping of a new world, that that talent can be used and that stake protected and the decision made.

We are not after all a new and inexperienced people. We have governed ourselves longer than any other people on earth. We have seen something of human history on this planet and we have drawn our own conclusions from what we have seen. We know what it is to want what the peoples of Asia want and the peoples of Africa and Europe. We know what can happen when the great currents of life break over the banks of the old restrictions and move out toward the future. We believe, on the basis of what we have seen in this world, that men, if they can, will move toward freedom: that the desire for freedom and fulfilment is the law of the life of men as the pull of the earth is the law of the life of things. We believe, therefore, that if this new great stirring of mankind is freed of its necessities the world will move toward us. And it is there, in that labor, not in an insane and ruinous war, that we believe the struggle will really be joined.

The paradox, then, resolves itself in that juncture. For if you believe, in spite of the squeaking ghosts, that life will go on in this earth, you prepare for life: you educate for life. Whatever your tongue may say your heart continues to believe and your actions are truer than your words. As this action here is truer than our words who take part in it—this action by which this college and this woman commit themselves once more to a belief in the free and creative future of mankind.

SPEECH AT MID-CENTURY [4]

HORACE G. RAHSKOPF [5]

Professor Horace G. Rahskopf, president of the Speech Association of America in 1950, gave this address at the opening session of the Mid-Century Convention of that organization in the Grand Ball Room, Hotel Commodore, New York City, on Thursday morning, December 28, 1950. Meeting with the Speech Association in this convention were the American Educational Theatre Association, the National University Extension Association, the National Thespian Society, and the National Society for the Study of Communication. The general theme of the convention during its three-day session, December 27-30, was "a mid-century reevaluation of our teaching and research." Some two thousand registered and several hundred were in the audience at this opening session.

Dr. Rahskopf's address stated clearly his progressive speech philosophy. The issues of the day, as Rahskopf treated them, were: (1) Is communication primarily a technological matter (concerned with machines)? (2) Should communication be taught primarily as a written procedure? Is writing more basic than speaking? (3) Are those trained in language and literature qualified to teach speech? (4) What place should speech have in the program of "general education"? (5) Have educators placed sufficient emphasis on the "Processes of face-to-face cooperative thinking on which democracy depends?" His answers involved a consideration of the nature of speech and its relation to public speaking, semantics, discussion, play production, and other special applications. He is forceful in delivery, precise in articulation, fluent, and at home with his numerous educational audiences.

Mr. Chairman, fellow presidents and colleagues in the teaching of speech: The mid-century is a time of great rejoicing for all of us in the Speech Association of America. This is our thirty-sixth anniversary. Since 1914 we have grown from seventeen founders to a membership of nearly six thousand. Our program, now carried on with an annual budget of more than $50,-000, involves extensive committee and organizational activities. Our research and educational publications are significant and

---

[4] Text and permission to reprint supplied through the courtesy of Dr. Horace Rahskopf.

[5] For biographical note, see Appendix.

growing in number; many of them have been developed in co-operation with other major educational groups. The range of our educational interests is now typified by the position of our Association as a department of the National Education Association and a constituent member of the American Council on Education, as well as by our affiliation through the Committee on Debate Materials with the National University Extension Association. We anticipate an even wider range of affiliations with major teaching and research groups at the national level. We also have close working relationships with flourishing affiliated and regional organizations representing the varied aspects of our broad field of human activity. The importance of speech in human life has probably never been more widely understood or greatly appreciated than it is at this hour. We have, therefore, a basis for optimism as we move forward into the second half of the twentieth century.

Nevertheless, we should not forget that our nation and the world exist in grave emergency. Pride of achievement is pleasant, but is also dangerous if it gives us a false sense of well-being. The vital question for us now is, How can we best serve the nation and the life of freedom? To that question, I invite your attention. The search for the best avenues of service will require frank recognition of our limitations and errors; and though I do not like to be a negative critic, I shall not speak softly.

We scarcely need to be told that the world crisis has intensified both the challenge and the opportunity for our profession. I want to discuss these challenges and the significance of these opportunities from three standpoints: first, from the standpoint of the world scene; second, from the standpoint of education in our own country; and third, from the standpoint of the place of speech in American education.

The world scene is obviously one of turmoil and confusion. Communism broods over us like a dark and vaporous cloud and infiltrates the atmosphere of freedom. In the council of nations communication between peoples is hindered by falsehood masquerading as truth. Some men suffer from the delusion that conflict is a fundamental process of human life and that violence is an ultimate means to power. Mankind seems not to have learned that persuasion is more lasting than violence and that the co-operative pooling of ideas is greater than either violence or persuasion. Self-interest befogs the landscape, narrows our vision, and clogs the channels of our communication.

Under such conditions free men have difficulty seeing clearly the path before them. We Americans are endangered not merely by power from abroad, but also by our own internal limitations and weaknesses. One of these weaknesses lies close to the main theme of our Convention at this mid-century: As a people we are deficient in the processes by which policy is formulated. We fumble and hedge; we quarrel among ourselves. Like the rest of mankind we, too, have served the gods of competition and conflict and have allowed them to hinder that meeting of minds on which democracy depends. In plain terms, we are deficient in communication. Here is one of the most serious weaknesses in our bastion of defenses for democracy.

The unpleasant truth is that education in America is partly responsible for this inaptitude of our people. The charge may sound extreme. Communication and speech have never received greater emphasis than they are given today; at least we are talking about them more than ever. Nevertheless, the deeper meanings of these processes are often distorted and neglected; in this hour of crisis we pay heavy toll for superficiality.

Is a bill of particulars necessary? We need only to look around us. First, some thinkers in this area are so preoccupied with the instruments for transmission of symbols that they fail to make careful examination of the symbols themselves. Is not communication often discussed as though it were primarily a technological matter? Yet the machines and the circuits are not communication nor even the symbols of communication.

Second, some of the curricula of our American schools give little hint that scholars have long recognized oral language as the primary form. The emphasis in teaching has been, and to a considerable extent still is, on writing. The importance of effective writing certainly cannot be questioned, but our emphasis in education should be on speech, the immediate, face-to-face medium by which men think and act together. In our schools the assumption is still made that any one trained in language and literature is therefore qualified to teach speech. This assumption and its corollary, that writing is more basic than speaking, are among the chief confusions of educational thought in our time. Even the concept of "language arts" has in actual practice often reduced speech to a kind of oral verbalism and has missed the larger implication that speech is man's basic symbolic medium for social and intellectual activity.

Third, many plans for "general education" do lip service to the importance of communication, but overlook the truth that speech is its primary form. We are amazed at the extent to which educational leaders have failed to observe the function of speech in social and intellectual life. Many of them have reduced speech to a narrow verbalistic or noisemaking process and have not understood that it is of the essence of our common humanity.

Finally, our educational system has been so permeated by verbalistic and elocutionary concepts of speech that our people have not fully learned to use the processes of face-to-face cooperative thinking on which democracy depends. Many of our students enter college and some of them graduate with the idea that speech is simply oral composition, or, worse yet, merely performance.

These are some random evidences of educational confusion in the area of communication where the fate of free institutions is now being settled. American education is fiddling at the job of teaching speech while the fires of misunderstanding and conflict threaten to destroy us.

We students and teachers of speech share responsibility for the muddled state of thinking about communication in our educational system. Let us glance at ourselves.

First, some of us apparently have not learned that cooperation is more fundamental than conflict. A few of us are still beating the tournament drums, priding ourselves on the number of contests engaged in and the number of decisions won. A very few of us are still using "smart" practices to win such decisions. The value of competition is undeniable; pro and con debating has an important place in modern life. Nevertheless, some of us have not seen competition and debating in their true perspective, and have not given the cooperative processes of discussion the emphasis which their social importance justifies. We must admit that some of the sins we have committed in the name of competition are a disgrace to education.

Second, many of us are uncertain what we mean by the term fundamentals of speech. In some of our colleges the course called "Fundamentals of Speech" is essentially a course in elementary public speaking, in other places essentially voice and diction. Some of our leading departments of speech have given up the attempt to offer a general introductory course and have established in its place a sequence of elementary courses in public speaking, voice and diction, and oral interpretation of literature. One of our most urgent needs is some agreement about what is fundamental in speech behavior.

Third, in like manner, many of us are not certain what we mean by elements of speech. Does that phrase refer to the various aspects of a speaker's action, or to the features of the setting of an act of speech, or to the different forms and uses of speech? Some uses of this term suggest all three of these meanings; and lists of the elements of speech, written by leading authorities in our field, include these different types of elements without discrimination. We need to systematize our analysis of speech behavior.

Fourth, some of us are not even sure what we mean by the term speech. One illustration of our confusion will serve. In the literature of our field I have seen the statement, "All speaking is public speaking." Now the obvious truth intended is that all speaking is social. Nevertheless, many a student and many a citizen will be puzzled and confused by the statement, especially if he has taken the trouble to observe that speech occurs not only as public speaking but also in such forms as conversation, discussion, reading aloud, and acting. His confusion will not be diminished by the fact that some of our best-known textbooks, whose declared purpose is to present a course of basic training in speech and not just in public speaking, are nevertheless primarily texts on public speaking. The talk given before a group may indeed be our readiest means of general speech improvement in a classroom situation; but that fact does not justify the blunt statement by some of our leaders that all speaking is public speaking. Even casual observation shows the utter nonsense of such an assertion. Are we really so confused and careless that we cannot clarify and systematize the distinction between speech as a basic human process and the various forms in which speech occurs? Our students and the public we serve have a right to expect clearer thinking from us.

Finally, some of us who teach speech have apparently not realized that our specialisms are but partial approaches to one great primary aspect of human life. We seem not to understand that our many different avenues of study and teaching—such as public speaking, oral interpretation, speech correction, and acting —are but different approaches to one great educational objective, i.e., the improvement of speech. To some of the specialists among us acting may seem closer to the dance, for example, than to voice science. Speech correction may seem closer to medicine than to rhetoric, oral interpretation closer to literature than to speech correction, and public speaking closer to the social sciences than to audiology. These relationships between aspects of the study of speech and other areas are real and important; they indicate the tremendous range of the speech field. Nevertheless, anyone who fully grasps the concept of speech as a basic social and cultural process of human life will also realize that our various educational activities in teaching public speaking, oral interpretation, radio speaking, acting, speech correction, and related processes, deal with the same distinctive kind of human behavior, and are varied means to the same goal, i.e., the improvement of our people's mastery of this unique human function called speech. Although our relations to other areas of study are of great importance, all of us who teach any phase of speech are dealing with the same quality of human life. We ought to recognize the common ground on which we stand.

The old familiar story of the blind men and the elephant is pertinent. Of course the elephant was in part like a tree, and in part like a rope, and in part like a spear. Each man was right, yet no one of them could see the real truth.

> And so these men of Indostan
> Disputed loud and long,
> Each in his own opinion
> Exceeding stiff and strong,
> Though each was partly in the right,
> And all were in the wrong!

We who insist that our specialisms are complete elephants are wrong; in our preoccupation with one aspect we are missing the larger truth and the wholeness of view on which our greatest usefulness depends.

What I have said may be summed up in three statements: (1) The world situation is confused and dangerous, partly if not primarily because men are deficient in their understanding and use of communication. (2) In education the attitudes toward speech reflect this misunderstanding and confusion. Many of our colleagues have not fully realized that speech is the primary form of communication, hence an integral part of our humanity. (3) We who concentrate on the study and teaching of speech share responsibility for these confusions because we have not fully systematized our own fundamental concepts and have allowed our special interests to limit our view of the task we share. These follies have intensified the dangers of this hour of crisis.

This, then, should be our theme at mid-century: Our primary job is the deepening and strengthening of the concepts on which all our study and teaching rest. This was a major need before the international emergency became acute; it is even more urgent now. Of course we shall do all we can to help meet the crisis. We are ready, even eager, to join our colleagues in other areas in planning the part of education in the emergency. We are ready, even eager, to contribute to military programs in whatever ways and to whatever extent may be necessary. We are ready, even eager, to help inform the public on the issues of the crisis. But underlying all these services is the need to define our field, to state our goals, and to develop our methods so clearly that no one of us will lose his way in the confusions of our time. The prophetic statement made by Rupert Cortright of Wayne University in the national crisis of 1942 still applies: "This may be the crisis in which we can fail, not by any backwardness in persuading others of the importance of speech, but because we ourselves are not prepared to meet the challenge. . . ." [6] The greatest need of our profession at this hour is the deeper probing and clarification of the principles on which we stand. These principles cannot be fabricated. They are inherent in our work and need only to be fully discovered and made effective.

We should keep constantly before us the truth that speech is more than public speaking, or conversation, or acting, or any other one of its forms or uses. It is deeper than its visible and audible aspects. Speech is a primary and unique aspect of life. The soundness of democracy among us depends on effective speech. Our diplomatic effectiveness abroad depends on effective speech. Our military effectiveness is conditioned largely by effective speech.

Speech is the essential pattern of behavior common to all the forms of speaking. Even casual observation reveals that conversation, discussion, addressing an audience, speaking to a microphone, reading aloud, acting, or story telling, are essentially alike. Of course differences exist among these activities, but the essential pattern of action occurs in every one of them. This fundamental process is speech.

We should recognize that such a concept is somewhat elusive. In one sense we never see or hear speech as such; we experience it only as one or another of its varied forms. If the concept of speech is to be made fully clear we shall have to define its common pattern of action. This may be done in two ways.

First, we may describe speech in terms of the essential phases of a speaker's behavior. The four traditional elements—thought, language, voice, and action—are familiar. I like to list them as five—social attitudes, thought processes, bodily movements, sounds, and words. Others have broken the elements of speech down in still different patterns. An essential truth often overlooked, however, is that no matter how broadly or minutely we describe the elements of speech they are as inseparable as the elements in a chemical union and as dynamic as the particles of an atom.

[6] Mimeographed letter to Sustaining Members of the Speech Association of America, May 21, 1942.

Again, the unique pattern which characterizes all speech may be described in terms of the setting. Every act of speech involves speaker, listener or listeners, time and place, a body of ideas, and a body of commonly understood symbolic processes. Speaking is an interaction among these elements. Again, the relationships are inseparable and dynamic. Speech is a distinctive and unified process of human life.

I summarize these well-known concepts here because they outline in skeleton form the whole subject matter of our field as well as the essential unity of our educational function. We teachers of speech are dealing with a primary aspect of human life; its importance cannot be overrated, especially in this time of emergency. There is little hope, however, that our colleagues in other disciplines or our fellow citizens will understand fully what we are trying to do until we ourselves have completed the task of defining our basic principles. Our most effective contribution to the cause of freedom depends upon a clear exposition of our subject and of our educational goals.

Our major goals lie not primarily in numbers or material growth, but in ideas; not in curricular units, but in educational concepts; not alone in the processes of persuasion, but even more in the cooperative integration of ideas; not in techniques primarily, but in the common humanity which binds us all together. Now at mid-century our main task is in the realm of basic philosophy. We must clarify and systematize the ideas that underlie, and unify our work. Our faith as educators demands it. The preservation of our freedom may depend on it.

A LOFTY PURPOSE SHARED [7]

JOHN EDWARD WALLACE STERLING [8]

Dr. John Edward Wallace Sterling delivered the following address on October 7, 1949, on the occasion of his inauguration as the fifth president of Stanford University. The speech was broadcast over Palo Alto and San Jose stations and later rebroadcast on the West Coast by NBC and CBS.

The inaugural address well lived up to the traditions of high scholarship and educational insight associated with this speaker. President Sterling, as a historian, interpreted, in view of the complex postwar world, the growth and present character of the American university, its newer problems and programs, and its specific ways of growth, through, for example, "collaborative testing" of its objectives, courses, and their "mutual relationships."

The address was first composed in longhand. The final draft was rewritten "many" times and revised after consultation with the staff and faculty. This precision in preparation was typical of Sterling's carefulness in his thinking and in his use of language.

The introduction was disproportionately long. President Sterling apparently wanted to create an atmosphere of friendliness before stating his ideas on the problems of the University.

The discourse was delivered from the manuscript with little or no deviation from the text. The speaker had had much radio experience as news analyst for the Columbia Broadcasting System from September 1942, to July 1948. During much of the time he had broadcast fifteen minutes, three to five times each week. He had covered the Republican National Convention in Chicago in 1944 and the United Nations Conference in San Francisco in 1945. This experience enabled him to make satisfactory adjustments in his timing and rate of delivery. His voice was pleasant, varied, and fully capable of projecting his ideas. "Whether by his radio experience or natural inclination, he speaks with few gestures and is accustomed to the necessity of staying near the microphone. The general impression is that of a friendly, sincere, and understanding man who is speaking to his friends".[9]

During the recent war I heard a broadcast by that distinguished reporter, Edward R. Murrow. He had gone along on an

---

[7] Text supplied through the courtesy of President Sterling.

[8] For biographical note, see Appendix.

[9] For these comments, the editor is indebted to Mr. David Grant, of California State Polytechnic College, formerly a graduate student in speech at Stanford University.

air mission over Germany and was describing the experience. The tension before take-off time seemed to be relaxed once he was air borne, but as the ship moved across German soil and nearer to the target it occurred to Mr. Murrow how much his courage would have been amplified if only he had been able to leave his stomach at home. The run over the target was made and the bombs released without misadventure. But the flak was heavy. One shell exploded, as Mr. Murrow thought, quite close to the ship and he said to the pilot, "Skipper, that one was pretty close." "Oh, no," responded the Skipper, "when they're really close you can smell 'em." This observation made no sense whatsoever to Mr. Murrow because, as he reported, he had been holding his breath for three hours.

The purpose for which you have been good enough to assemble here today and the peace and beauty of this setting are far removed from the context of war. But I must say that my stomach and breath control are not unaffected by the occasion. For I am deeply sensitive to what is visible and audible in this ceremony and to its symbolism as well.

The Board of Trustees of Stanford University, speaking through its president, Mr. Paul Edwards, has now formally charged me with the responsibility of providing the University with that leadership which resides in the office of president. This responsibility I now formally accept. I shall discharge it with integrity, always, and with such talent and energy as I possess.

I accept this responsibility with pride. I am proud to be one of that noble company of men and women whose business is education, and I am proud to be associated with this University.

I accept my responsibilities also with humility, a sentiment by no means irreconcilable with the pride I have confessed. I have read something of Stanford's history. It has not been untroubled by adversities and disappointments. But it is essentially the story of strong growth from good soil and, as any person is enhumbled in the presence of greatness, so am I in the knowledge of what has been accomplished here. Many hands have labored to produce this accomplishment, and the work continues. The University boasts a Board of Trustees of distinguished citizens of broad experience, a faculty of great scholars and teachers, a student body of high standing, always proud of its honor code and in this autumn season wondering whether the cycle of lean and lush years that Joseph saw in Pharaoh's dream might have any relationship to what is now our chief Saturday preoccupation. The University is also fortunate in the strong loyalty of its alumni whose interest in their alma mater is deep rooted, and whose support grows in generosity with each passing year. I bow in respect and admiration for all that these members and friends of the Stanford family, past and present, have done and are doing.

Indeed, the president of a university is surrounded by so much knowledge in the heads of his faculty and so much practical experience in his board of trustees, alumni, and student body that he is in constant danger of assuming that whatever he says will be transmuted by the chemistry of complacency into the distillation of wisdom. If he can escape the consequences of this occupational disease, he is in a singularly fortunate position to learn from those with whom he works and to apply the essence of what he learns in the making of university policy. To this I pledge you my heart and mind.

You will have noticed that I have been accompanied here not only by representatives from Stanford's Board of Trustees, faculty, alumni, and student body, but also by representatives of other universities, colleges, and institutions of learning. They honor Stanford by their presence. They are here in accordance with the custom of having such a convocation to mark academic launchings of this sort. With their indulgence and with the indulgence of all mariners, I would suggest that they are the academic equivalent of the traditional champagne, but in this case, champagne of a very rare vintage indeed. But they constitute much more than that. They symbolize the existence and common purpose within this nation of a spirited and independent community of higher learning without which the march of our civilization would grind to an ignominious halt. Stanford is honored to have so many of them and their institutions represented here today.

Universities are confronted today with responsibilities of unprecedented magnitude. I should like to explore with you briefly this afternoon a few matters pertaining to these responsibilities and to the opportunities associated with them. Since I am an historian by inclination and training, I think of these matters from the historian's viewpoint. I am struck by two things. The first is the obvious and overwhelming fact of change and growth of institutions of higher education during the last seventy-five years and especially in our own time. The second is that even more rapid and profound changes have taken place in the world for which the universities have the obligation to give leadership and nourish leaders. In the midst of this mighty changing world the universities must first devise and use methods to understand the nature of these changes and what causes them. The universities then have the further obligation to communicate their methodology and the substance of their investigations to their members and to the national community.

University development during the past hundred years has been marked by certain emphases. Oxford and Cambridge, in their nineteenth-century heyday, placed emphasis on the production of good citizens, on the training of an elite to assure leadership in public affairs and the learned professions. The purpose was to familiarize selected young people with "the best that has been thought and said in the world" so that successive generations would be bound together through the sharing of a common intellectual estate. This education was general rather than specialized and thus differed from that of a technical college, a research institute, or a graduate school of specialization.

A second type of university emphasis I would mention is that which holds that investigation is more important than instruction and that learning for learning's sake is the proper business of the university. Stress is placed on the advancement rather than the communication—or, as some have suggested, the embalmment—of knowledge. This emphasis was conspicuous in German universities during the nineteenth century. It attached fundamental importance to an academic freedom which would permit members of university faculties to follow the evidence produced by investigation to honest and ultimate conclusions. Their attitude toward contemporary controversies of the workaday political and economic world was essentially one of neutrality, and they believed that this attitude accorded with the canons of scholarship by which they worked. Associated with this emphasis and attitude, if not deriving from it, was the view that the student also should share this freedom in choice and initiative, that his academic menu, as Professor Morrison has put it, should be à la carte. This view, of course, has produced the elective system.

The influence of this second emphasis has been far reaching. It has been strongly reflected in university development in this country during the past seventy-five years and has done much to increase the stature of American universities. Oxford and Cambridge in their turn have been affected by it and have adjusted much to its impact.

But universities, like other institutions, are affected by changing conditions and pressures. Just as the first emphasis has been modified by the second, so now the second is feeling the pressure of circumstance. The past several years have witnessed the generation of major forces with which universities are having to reckon. The first of these is the almost meteoric rise of applied science and technology. To a remarkable degree, technological achievements have caught and fired the public imagination. The general public has never been particularly interested in the reasoning of the pure scientist or the severe discipline of his method or in his learning for learning's sake, but it has become immensely intrigued by the practical results which flow from his discoveries. The public's interest is, if I may paraphrase Macaulay, not so much in making men perfect as in making imperfect human beings comfortable. Its hero, as another observer puts it, "is the man who makes two blades of grass grow where one grew before," who has a sense that

> something from his hand has power
> To live and act and serve the future hour.

A second force with which universities now have to reckon derives from the democratization of society, a process that is roughly contemporaneous with the rise of applied science. This phenomenon of democratization manifests itself in the larger number of students that have been and are seeking admission to universities. They come in greater numbers for a variety of reasons; but not least of all because of the widely held conviction that a university education for the greatest possible number is appropriate to an epoch which is seeking to achieve a juster social order. The accent of this epoch is plebeian rather than patrician. Its tendency is to repudiate in education preferment for the social uppercrust and to repudiate equally the cult of aloof ivory-tower detachment and dispassionate neutrality which sought its justification in learning for learning's sake. This force is real and strong and omnipresent. And its existence presents to the universities of a free society one of the greatest challenges in the history of education.

One other force I would mention. The United States has in the last few decades achieved a position of high eminence among the nations of the world. It is a nation "conceived in liberty and dedicated to the proposition that all men are created equal." In a context much broader today than that in which Lincoln spoke, the question is still being asked "whether that nation or any nation so conceived and so dedicated can long endure."

It has been our traditional view that the state existed for the purpose of making men free to develop their faculties and that its power is and should be limited. It has also been our traditional view that a democratic state is and should be one in which conflicting opinions have free play, and in which government is made to accept the proper responsibility of explaining itself to its electorate.

These traditional views are in my estimation still valid. Yet they are today placed under heavy strain. The age we live in has witnessed the aggrandizement of state power and the extension and ramification of its activities. It has witnessed, too, a growing complexity of life. There seems to be no end to public issues—domestic and international—nor any end to the spate of comment on each of them. Not only our understanding but our patience as well is frequently taxed to the point where we feel like crying with Job,

> How long will ye vex my soul,
> And break me in pieces with words.

But we cannot traduce our own terms. We cannot escape the conditions we set for ourselves. If freedom of speech is fundamental to our system, then freedom of speech it should be, however opinions may conflict. The problem thus posed is one of discrimination and discernment. Most of us are, as individuals, normally articulate; a few abnormally so. But as social groups, we do more listening than talking. How are we as listeners or readers to distinguish gold from dross? Our democratic system can operate successfully only when our teachers, business leaders, and political representatives know "not merely that they will be held to account for what they do, but that those who hold them to account can weigh facts and reflect upon their meaning."

Today, education is being anxiously and sincerely charged with the task of equipping citizens for the exercise of this civic responsibility. Colleges and universities are expected to shoulder their large share of this undertaking. In carrying out this undertaking the universities have the duty to bar any short cuts by which the state lays down for the citizen "articles of unexamined belief." A state that fears to encourage independent thought does not trust itself. "A state," said John Stuart Mill, "which dwarfs its men in order that they may be more docile implements in its hands even for beneficial purposes will find that with small men no great thing can be accomplished."

Thus, you see, a university is today supposed to perform a variety of educational services, or if you prefer, miracles. First, it is supposed to train young people for life's work. This includes training for professional careers (and I may say that in this area the universities are reputed to have done a commendable job); it includes also, I dare say, training for careers that are undetermined when the training occurs. In this area the training is not so readily evaluated.

Second, the universities are expected to discover and organize knowledge. That is to say, they are expected to have learning pursued for learning's sake. Here their record is excellent, for they have in large measure fashioned twentieth century civilization, especially material civilization, as we know it. They have made us extremely conscious of the place of science in our lives.

Third, they are expected through general education to inculcate a sense of values according to which the gifts of material civilization · can be wisely judged and intelligently used. They are likewise expected to equip young men and women to exercise constructively their responsibilities as citizens.

And fourth, the universities are expected to do all of these things for more students than ever before.

Can the universities live up to these expectations? If they are to do so, two things are certainly necessary: Taxpayer and benefactor alike must be prepared to foot large bills, and second, the universities must continuously take stock of themselves.

The problem of large enrollments is a real one. Universities are not opposed to the democratization of education which produces large numbers of students; they are merely dazed by it. Their facilities, human and material, have been overtaxed and a high quality of education has thus been placed in some jeopardy. But if facilities can keep pace with enrollments, great gains would be brought in prospect for our democratic system by a raising of the general level of education.

But the burden of expanding facilities must be largely borne by tax-supported institutions, if for no other reason than that the multiplication of privately endowed facilities will be difficult in this era of exalted taxation.

Furthermore, the privately endowed institutions have a role of their own to play. By their number and individuality they lend variety to our whole higher educational system. By their very nature they have greater opportunity and responsibility to experiment and thus to stimulate improvement, not only among themselves, but also among their larger, tax-supported sister institutions.

As to the balance that is to be struck between those curricula which prepare students for specific professions and advanced study and those which provide for a general education, I dare say each college and university will have to work out its own solution. Of recent years there has been a tendency to require in the first two college years subjects presumed to provide a general education and to permit concentration on major interests in the second two years. Such a tendency would seem to fit well into the growing junior college movement, and it has much to commend it. But my plea here is that such an arrangement shall not be regarded merely as a set of requirements to be met and discharged en route to specialization. For we must bear in mind that the current revitalized interest in general education is part of a deeply felt need to prepare young people for the responsibilities of citizenship. We have gone far with our methods for accumulating and dispensing facts. We have not gone as far as we can and should go with our methods for producing understanding.

It will be cogently and properly argued that for the great majority of our youth even two years' experience at the college level is a gain of great value, and I should agree. It will be argued also that for this great majority who cannot manage a college and university education, it is important in high school and junior college to equip them, not only with a sense of civic responsibility, but also with skills that they may use to earn bread and butter, and here too I should agree. But to me, education at any level is a great treasure. I should hope that every young person in this country would have the opportunity to go as far in education as his talent can carry him. And I should urge that it is society's responsibility to provide such opportunity and to provide it without any coercion to fit a pattern.

But also I should hope that talent, and the industry which fortifies it, would be sternly tested at critical points along the way, more sternly perhaps than it now is, so that the opportunity which society provides will be appreciated by those who stand to benefit from it, and so that we may learn where our potential for advanced work and leadership resides. It is with this potential that college and university education should be particularly concerned. Any society, not least of all a democratic society, will serve itself badly if it fails to exact high standards for higher education. Provided that such testing can identify this potential, even more clearly than now, colleges and universities should be in an improved position to discharge their responsibilities.

But how are they at their educational level in a democratic and industrial society to implant a wide culture, such as some of the older institutions once imparted through the medium of the classics? To this question the universities have not as yet provided a strong answer. One step has been taken, as I have already indicated, through a revitalized interest in general education. But this interest as yet lacks dynamics.

During the past thirty years, the Communist and Nazi movements have sharply changed the course of history. The philosophies which inspired them were positive and dynamic and, being so, they have placed the philosophy of democracy under challenge to meet these qualities. This challenge has evoked in this country widespread and understandable apprehension. I hope that in our concern over what totalitarianism may do to our ideals of education for free men, we shall not lose sight of the danger that lurks in what we ourselves may do to these ideals under the stimulus of fear. To protect ourselves against this form of self-destruction and to equip ourselves with confidence in the future, I urge recognition of the fact that the essence of our American democracy is the promise of growth. "Democracy," as Raymond Fosdick puts it, "is not a finished product"; it has not been "handed down from some political Sinai. Democracy is . . . a conception of human relations rooted in the worth and dignity of the individual and inspired by the developing idea of freedom."

The universities, it seems to me, can more effectively aid in the realization of democracy's promise if they will apply to themselves a method which recently served this nation so well. During the war there existed an activity called Operations Research. Its purpose was to study the operations of war itself. It began by calling into question the major objectives, and each part of every strategy and tactic. It was based on the principles of freedom of research, freedom of thought, freedom of communication of ideas. It was collaborative.

The problems of higher education are not the problems of war. But if universities are to develop curricula and instruction which will impart to students an understanding of the culture they inherit, they must apply to their own operations, better than in the past, the principles and methods of Operations Research. After all, these are nothing more than the principles and methods applied by university scholars in their respective fields of specialization. A collaborative testing of our educational objectives, of the content of courses, and of their mutual relationships will be of great and necessary value in the formulation of educational policy and in determining methods of operation. And if we are to relate all this to the promise of growth which inheres in our democracy, we must have as a prime educational objective the development in student and teacher alike of a greater capacity "to make relevant judgments and to discriminate among values." For only through these can the abjectness of tyranny be exposed, the measure of material things taken and the basic worth of individual freedom appraised.

Our educational gains in the last half century have been conspicuously identified with material progress. For these gains I have nothing but the highest praise, but they supply us with only one part of the equipment we need today. Education has enabled men to take the measure of many things. Its preeminent task today is to enable him to take his own measure—his own moral measure, and the moral measure of the society of which he is a part.

RELIGION

RELIGION—A PROP FOR THE WEAK? [1]

HAROLD C. PHILLIPS [2]

The Reverend Harold C. Phillips, minister of the First Baptist Church, Cleveland, Ohio, preached this sermon at the Riverside Church, New York, on Sunday, January 29, 1950. Dr. Phillips, as teacher and sermonizer, is a representative preacher of the Middle West. He belongs to that coterie of outstanding Baptist preachers of which Dr. Harry Emerson Fosdick is the most notable living representative.

What were the characteristics of this sermon by Dr. Phillips? (1) It is based on a text. (2) The theme is illustrated with Biblical citations. (3) The sermon is well constructed. Its three-fold division is obvious, and the details of the outline are clear. (4) The introduction and conclusion are designed to impress the audience. (5) The sentences are simple, and the language is never unduly formal, academic, or abstract. (6) The theme is personal and directly inspirational rather than social or political in its emphasis. (7) The religious philosophy in this discourse is progressive but not ultra-liberal. The speaker here is more interested in personal religion than in theological exposition.[3]

Phillips attended Doane Academy, then preparatory school of Denison University. He was a member of the Cicero debating society and for each of four successive years was on the winning debate team against the Irving society. He also debated at Denison and preached in a country church. At Union Theological Seminary he had training in voice under Francis Carmody, a New York lawyer. He also had training in interpretative reading under S. S. Curry, of Boston, formerly president of the Curry School of Expression.

Dr. Phillips states: "I suppose the first prerequisite of an effective speech is the sincerity and unselfconsciousness of the speaker. A course in public speaking would no doubt be of great value to one in helping him overcome awkwardness of gesture and the improper use of his voice, but I question if it is a substitute for the sort of unselfconsciousness which comes, as I think, from having something to say and saying it." [4]

---

[1] Text supplied by Dr. Harold C. Phillips and permission given for this reprinting through the courtesy of the author.

[2] For biographical notes, see Appendix.

[3] *Representative American Speeches: 1944-1945*, p291-2.

[4] Letter to this editor, April 14, 1950.

"For when I am weak, then am I strong."—II Corinthians
12:10

We are to consider today one of the criticisms sometimes
made of the Christian religion. In substance it is that Christianity is a prop for the weak. It is therefore that to which
strong, healthy, virile folk need not pay much attention. Such
people do not need the Christian religion since they are quite
self-sufficient. Weak people need Christianity but not strong
people; sick people but not healthy people; people in distress
or trouble need Christianity but not those upon whose path the
sun shines and good fortune smiles. Even as a man in good
health can pass up the doctor and pass by the hospital, so the
strong can pass up the church. Religion is a sort of crutch
for the crippled. But healthy people do not need crutches, they
can get along by their own strength, proceed under their own
steam.

That this attitude has created a bad psychology towards
religion is evident. I remember that when an undergraduate I
felt not a little embarrassment in letting it be known that I was
studying for the Christian ministry. I should not have been
embarrassed in telling anyone that I was taking up medicine,
law, engineering, going into business or the like. But that a
normal, healthy, red-blooded young man should go into the
ministry—well, that just did not seem normal. The bad psychology appears also in that in the minds of some people religion is regarded as a sort of feminine interest. How often has
it been said that Mr. So-and-so has his religion in his wife's
name. As the little jingle has it:

> In the world's broad field of battle
> In the bivouac of life,
> Here we see the Christian soldier,
> Represented by his wife.

Well now what shall we say to this opinion? I suppose the
first observation to be made is that since the world is so full,
well-nigh "bursting at the seams," with crippled people who
have come to the end of their rope we ought to be glad that
this prop is available for them at least. Has there ever been an

age in which there were so many depressed people, discouraged people, disheartened people, displaced people, at their wits' end as there are today? If the Christian religion then is nothing more than a resource for those in trouble, let us be thankful for it, for we do live in a troubled world full of troubled people.

We do not as a rule need help in getting into trouble, but most of us need help in getting out of it, and if the gospel affords that help let us be grateful that it is available for those who need it. For it is perfectly astonishing what Christianity has done *to* people, *with* people, *for* people in trouble or need. The Bible bears full testimony to this. "God is our refuge and strength, a very present help in trouble." A man who felt defenseless wrote that. "The Lord is my shepherd; I shall not want." A man who felt privation wrote that. "I can do all things through Christ which strengtheneth me." A man who felt his weakness wrote that. Such statements are typical.

Consider Paul. He stated the matter once in a paradox. Said he, "When I am weak, then am I strong." He had what he called "a thorn in the flesh, the messenger of Satan to buffet me." "Most gladly," he said, "will I rather glory in my infirmities, that the power of Christ may rest upon me. Therefore I take pleasure in infirmities, in reproaches, in necessities, in persecutions, in distresses for Christ's sake: for when I am weak, then am I strong." Now I submit that it is a great deal better for a man to say, "When I am weak, then am I strong," than to have to say, "When I am weak, then am I licked." If the Christian religion can take a man like Paul, possessed of some infirmity that threatens his vitality and usefulness, and so empower him that instead of being broody or embittered, instead of spending his days worrying about his health, feeling his pulse, marooned in self-pity, he goes forth inspired, undiscouraged, unconquerable, then let us sincerely pray that more people, conscious of their weakness or limitations, will use Christianity as a prop. For there is in religion this power which can give "beauty for ashes, the oil of joy for mourning, and the garment of praise for the spirit of heaviness."

But now in the second place let us look with a little more discernment at this question of human weakness and strength.

Who are the weak? Who are the strong? Here we confront a strange paradox. The weak actually turn out at times to be the strong, and the strong the weak. The weak often win out while the strong lose out. It very often happens that out of recognized and confessed human weakness some of the greatest blessings of life have come, while from our alleged strength has come some of the most diabolical and disastrous of life's evils.

Consider human weakness. Is it not true that some of the very brightest pages of history have been written by those who like Paul have had some thorn in the flesh, some conscious limitation or handicap which has threatened to impede if not quite block their progress? It is a familiar fact that Beethoven was so deaf when he wrote some of his greatest works that he never heard them. It is also true that some of our great artists have had defective eyesight. An astonishing number of the world's great orators have had to overcome, as did Demosthenes, grave speech defects. Immanuel Kant was afflicted through all his life with a constricted chest that kept him in almost constant pain. But he wrote, "While I felt oppressed in my chest, my head was clear." Such illustrations could be multiplied endlessly. "Would Steinmetz, with his grossly deformed body, have developed his mind to such extraordinary uses had he been an Apollo?"

Now it will not do to say that such people achieved distinction in spite of their handicaps. It would probably be more fair to say that they achieved because of their handicaps. Adler, the psychologist, says that the greatest human achievements are won at precisely those points where individuals have to struggle most manfully. Perhaps then when Paul said, "When I am weak, then am I strong," he was stating a principle that is widely true. For out of human weakness, accepted, wrestled with and mastered, have come some of life's choicest values. It is an old saying that the poets learn in suffering what they teach in song.

But now consider human strength. It is a curious fact of life that some of the most disastrous evils that stalk the world, personal and social, come out of man's alleged strength. "It is one of the ironies of life that a man's worst calamities result, almost always, from his advantages. . . ." They grow not out of his recognized and acknowledged weakness but out of his supposed strength. If Paul could say, "When I am weak, then am I strong," we could well nigh say, "Where I am strong, there am I weak."

Take an illustration from the old Edinburgh castle. Only once in the history of Scotland was it ever captured. And this is how it happened. The castle had a weak spot. Defenders guarded that spot. But the defenders thought that on one side the steepness of the rock made the castle inaccessible and impregnable and so they put no sentries there. In the gray mist of an early morning a little party crept up that strong, unguarded, precipitous slope and surprised the garrison into surrender. You see, the defenders guarded the weak spot of the castle and so where the castle was weak, there it was strong; but the approaches they knew were strong, these they just forgot about, neglected, and so as it turned out, where the castle was strong, there it was weak.

That is so often the story of human life. Whenever a man falls it is usually at the point where he thinks he is strong. A man's moral weakness is well nigh invariably his strong point that goes unguarded. His bad point is his good point that slobbers over. The worst aspects of a man's life are usually the potentially best in him that get out of hand. Like Saul he falls on his own sword. His strength becomes his undoing.

For example, see how true this is of certain admirable qualities. Take self-confidence — surely an admirable trait. We all admire a man who walks up to a situation with sure step rather than with shaky knees and cold sweat. Yet have you stopped to think how easily self-confidence becomes self-conceit, how self-assurance becomes arrogance and pride? So out of strength comes weakness.

Or consider ambition. That, too, is a worthy quality. We admire the man who likes to get on, to make a success, to get to the top, and all that sort of thing. Yet how easily can ambition make a man avaricious and proud, how quickly can ambition convert a man into a hard-driving "go-getter" who has no time for worship, for friendship, for music, for good books, for the little amenities and courtesies of life—no time to live!

He gets to the top, but what of it? "What shall it profit a man, if he shall gain the whole world, and lose his own soul?"

Sympathy is an admirable trait. Some people are just naturally friendly, kindly, human, and most of their problems grow out of just that fact. For how easily does sympathy degenerate into maudlin sentimentality. Sympathy can convert a man into a sort of Old Faithful, always gushing, oozing. Indeed, sympathy may even make one incapable of serving people. For there are times when the best service we may render others is not by speaking soft, sweet words but strong, even hard words— "Son of man, stand upon thy feet, and I will speak unto thee." Sometimes the best service we can render is not that of the nurse who comes to fix our pillows and make us comfortable but of a doctor who says, "Get out of bed, put on your clothes, and get going!" But the sympathetic man at times cannot say that.

I suppose if I were to ask, "What value do we cherish most?" we would say, "Our freedom." We love freedom more than money—and that is saying a good deal. Twice in our lifetime have the freedom-loving nations of the world poured out unstintedly of their treasure, well nigh bankrupted their economy to defend freedom. We love it more than we love our life. Millions have chosen death that liberty might live. Most of us would rather die like men than live like slaves. Here then is our strong point.

Yet, whether you consider freedom politically or spiritually the plain truth is that some of the most shocking evils of our life today come from the abuse of this very freedom we treasure. There is an old saying that the best thing is the worst thing when the thing goes bad. And liberty, the best thing, easily degenerates into license—the worst thing. Indeed, I wonder if John Burroughs was not right when he said, "The vices, crimes, follies and excesses of society are the riot and overflow of its virtues. The pride of the rich, the tyranny of power, the lust of gain, the riot of sensuality are all a little too much of a good thing. . . ."

Of course this truth applies not only to individuals but to our world. Just where lies the danger to man today? Does it lie in his weakness? No, in his strength. Does his danger come from his ignorance? No, from his knowledge. Does our peril come from the fact that we do not know how to wage bacteriological warfare, to build rocket planes, or more atomic bombs? No, but from the fact that we do know. The evils that started World War I and II did not come from a Germany that was weak but from a Germany that was strong. Japan and Italy started aggressive wars and were destroyed not because they were weak but because they were strong. If there should be a World War III, which God forbid, whence will it come? More than likely out of misunderstandings and unresolved tensions between Russia and the United States. Is it just a coincidence that these two nations are regarded as the two strongest nations in the world today? Ah, Paul, you are right: "When I am weak, then am I strong." And history proves the reverse is true: "Where I am strong, there am I weak." As Dr. Fosdick has said, "The idea that we are made great by our superiorities and ruined by our inferiorities is a dangerous half truth."

Now it follows in the third place that in the fact that out of our strength comes our weakness lies man's undying need of God. For here man faces his dilemma, the paradox of his earthly life; namely, that in many instances he never is so insufficient as when he thinks he is sufficient. The evils of his personal life grow out of those very qualities that are potentially admirable. It may not be too much to say with John Burroughs that in some fashion his vices grow out of his virtues. The very power by which he seeks to make himself secure becomes the main cause of his insecurity. The very knowledge on which he depended—as he said with Mr. H. G. Wells that civilization was a race between education and catastrophe—this very knowledge, unless illumined and directed by the wisdom from above, is potentially able to destroy him and all his works.

Whence comes this paradox? What does this mean? The answer in theological language is that man is ensnared and imperilled by his sin. Paul expressed this truth well: "I see another law in my members, warring against the law of my mind, and bringing me into captivity to the law of sin. . . . O wretched man that I am! who shall deliver me from the body of this death?" One thing is certain: man cannot deliver himself from this dilemma. He is as it were mired in the morass of his own inner inconsistencies and contradictions, and his struggle to extricate himself by himself sends him deeper into the mire. It is impossible, for example, as Dr. John Baillie once pointed out, for a proud man by his own efforts to overcome his pride, since he would be proud of having done so and would thus fall victim to the worst pride of all—spiritual pride. There is even such a thing as being proud of your humility, as is evidenced in an autobiographical work published in 1930 in which occurs this sentence: "I have never lost the childlike humility which characterizes all truly great men."

Christianity a prop for the weak? Perchance behind this criticism lies a deep truth. Maybe it is! For if truth be told we are all weak. We are all finite, sinful mortals "standing in the need of prayer," and none so weak as those who think they are strong. Those who know they are weak and seek the divine aid, in their weakness are made strong; and those who know it not but are deluded by pride and self-sufficiency are exposed *and expose mankind* to the gravest dangers. For human strength unillumined by the divine wisdom, unguarded by the divine power, undirected by the divine spirit, unredeemed by God's grace, such strength today is man's greatest liability.

It was so in the first century. It was unregenerate power that crucified Christ the Truth, and it is the same unredeemed power that has been responsible for most of the crosses ever since, whether those crosses stand in the costly and cruel camaraderie of some Flander's Field or in the solitary splendor of some Calvary.

Our gospel is that in Calvary the problem of human life finds its only adequate solution. Here the paradox is resolved. For in Calvary man's sin confronts God's forgiving love. Calvary reveals not only unredeemed human power at its lowest and worst but the outgoing, redemptive power of God who in Christ is able to deliver man from this inner perversion from which he is unable to free himself. "O wretched man that I am! who shall deliver me from the body of this death?"—this inner contradiction that makes my strength my undoing? The answer of the Christian faith is: "Thanks be to God, who gives us the victory through our Lord Jesus Christ."

THE CHALLENGE OF COMMUNISM [5]

CHARLES H. MALIK [6]

Dr. Charles H. Malik, Minister of the Legation of Lebanon, and Lebanon's delegate to the United Nations, gave this address before the Chicago Council on Foreign Relations, at the Congress Hotel, Chicago, on December 14, 1950. Mr. Dagget Harvery, president of the Council, presided.

This speech, coming in the midst of the current and endless disputations at the current session of the United Nations at Lake Success, New York, over the labeling of Chinese aggression in Korea and kindred problems, was a distinct and clear contribution to the issue of communism versus western civilization.

Dr. Malik, a Christian (Greek Orthodox) Arab, graduate of the American University, Beirut, with an M.A. and Ph.D. from Harvard, had been a professor of philosophy at the American University from 1937 until his appointment as envoy extraordinary and minister plenipotentiary of the Republic of Lebanon to the United States in 1945. He had also served on various committees of the United Nations and had been the Lebanon delegate to the General Assembly of the United Nations beginning with the first session in 1946. During 1950-51 he fulfilled various speaking engagements throughout the United States.

His training, racial and religious, and his political background enabled him to define and expound better than most American interpreters the problem and solution of the communistic doctrine and program. The speech placed communism historically and currently in its setting of atheism, Marxism, relativism, nationalism, materialism, economic collectivism, statism; and explained the method and scope of its propagandistic appeal. Dr. Malik indicated the possible choices open to the Western world in reacting to the Russians and their doctrine. His solution (balance of power; economic, social, and political justice to the world, including the Orient; balance of mind, the equality in accessibility of truth and information; and balance of spirit) is comprehensive and constructive.

Dr. Malik speaks rapidly, almost passionately. Although he followed his manuscript at this Chicago conference, he is skillful in extemporaneous debate. A question period followed. He has vocal readiness, ample

[5] Text is from the *Christian Century*. 68:74-7, January 17, 1951. Permission for this reprint was given through the courtesy of Charles H. Malik, of the Legation of Lebanon, at Washington, D.C.; the Chicago Council on Foreign Relations, Louise Leonard Wright, Director; and the *Christian Century*, Chicago, Illinois.

[6] For biographical note, see Appendix.

English vocabulary, and a wealth of intellectual resourcefulness as demonstrated in the 1950-51 sessions of the United Nations.

States Dr. Malik, "In almost every case I write my speeches in advance in full. In running debates in the United Nations, however, I usually speak extemporaneously." [7]

Communism is originally a doctrine about reality, an ideal, and a call to action. Today, however, it has transported itself into the domain of concrete reality. For communism is now the principle of being of a great power and of a solidly organized group of nations under its hegemony. It is also the ideal and cause of a world-wide movement. It controls the life of about one third of the globe, formally and directly. At least another one third of the world determines its ultimate policies in terms of communism, albeit negatively and by way of reaction. Thus between themselves, the Communist and the non-Communist camps—both equally, though in opposite ways, functions of communism—constitute the totality of the effective agents of today's world.

What a difference, then, between the reality of communism today, which affects the life of the whole world, and the reality of communism a hundred years ago, when it was, to all appearance, no more than a bold cry in the wilderness. When Marx and Engels launched their wild attack on all known and existing patterns of life, the opening words of their "Manifesto"—"A specter is haunting Europe—the specter of communism"—were by no means a description of an existing situation; but today, exactly a century later, these same words are more than completely fulfilled. It may indeed have been only a specter then; but today the specter has taken on formidable concretion.

And yet, the dangers latent in communism need not have awaited the developments of this whole century to be fully realized; they were already there, in the pages of the "Manifesto," for the whole world to read, decades before communism had at its disposal the world's most highly organized war machinery.

At the outset of the two half-centuries that have just elapsed, men failed to realize the full character and magnitude of the

[7] Letter to this editor, March 8, 1951.

challenge of communism mainly because their sight was concentrated on the political and the quantitative. Due to its infinitesimal physical dimensions, the spiritual significance of communism simply eluded men's vision. Those who did read aright the signs of the times—and they were very rare: solitary and suffering figures like Nietzsche, Kierkegaard and Dostoievsky—did so because their vision penetrated beyond the outward dimension of events and grasped their inner spiritual and intellectual significance. Today, however, those who see only the political, social, economic and military threat of communism miss its true challenge as pathetically as did their predecessors. For both of them see out of focus; both are so impressed by the physical weakness or strength of what is essentially a spiritual revolution that they lose sight of its real character.

Communism is a thoroughly consistent system of thought. From its basic and initial metaphysical premises, its all-comprehensive materialistic conception of reality, to its interpretation of human-social-historical reality, dominated by historical economic determinism, to its amoral view of human action, determined in its motives, directions and worth only by its serviceability to the cause of world revolution, communism presents the spectacle of a tightly knit, rigid system of thought, permeated through and through, in its presuppositions, structure and conclusions, by the spirit of metaphysical monism, ethical and axiological relativism, self-centered, autonomous humanism, impersonalist collectivism, historical dynamism, and militant atheism.

Communism is predicated on the emphatic rejection of God. The whole order of the spirit is rejected; self-subsistent spiritual beings are denied, while the spirituality of corporeal beings, like man, is reduced to a function of their physical, biological and at best social existence. The Communist denial of God and the spirit is militant. Communism goes beyond agnosticism, beyond passive atheism; it assumes the form of aggressive and militant atheism. For God is not merely an illusion, but a harmful illusion, ingeniously utilized by priests and bourgeoisie for their own interests, and therefore combated by communism in the name of the class interests of the proletariat.

With the abolition of God goes the abolition of the absolute in any form. There is no absolute truth which man seeks and knows. There is no absolute good which man strives for, which eternally judges of man's actions and intentions and very being. Everything is relative—in its origin, being but a product of the material conditions of human existence, as well as in its form and function, being always subordinate to the interests and desires of classes. The good, the true, the beautiful, thus relativized, are ruthlessly subjectivized beyond any hope for a healthy, corrective relation to an objective order above the whims and interests of man.

The conception of man in communism is accordingly disfigured. Severed from his divine origin and divine destiny; denied the spiritual principle which gives his reason access to the truth, which endows his conscience and will with the craving for the good, which empowers his heart to love; imprisoned hopelessly in this world of strife and frustration, here to center all his hopes and here to erect his paradise—Communist man, thus despiritualized and depersonalized to the highest degree, is pathetically dehumanized. He is but a passing shadow of no duration, a fragment of no intrinsic or ultimate worth, a function of the striving of his generation for a more productive existence. Man's natural and inalienable rights are thus superseded by privileges bestowed by the collective; man's personal, intrinsic dignity is made to rest upon and emanate from his status in and contributions to the community; man's freedom—freedom of thought, freedom of being, freedom of self-achievement—is rendered conditional upon and utterly subservient to the whims and the interests of society.

From the point of view of world peace, what is important about this doctrine is its entrenchment as the official monolithic philosophy of one of the two great powers of the world today. This power, whose capital is Moscow, has inherited the vast realms of the former Russian empire, including its autocratic totalitarian organization. It has annexed to itself further millions of square miles and further hundreds of millions of human beings. Marx and his followers gloried in the fact that they were not only describing history: they were determined to take history into their hands and change it. Next to the bourgeoisie, it was the philosophers who mainly described events from the outside who were the targets of the Communists' sharpest shafts of ridicule. From the very beginning communism was one of the crassest lusts for power the world has ever known.

The actual, historical, political enshrinement of communism in the Russian Soviet state meant a total concentration of all origination in the hands of the government. Everything flows from and is licensed by the government. Thus there are no independent free sources of thought, creation, activity: the assumption being, as Mr. Acheson remarked not long ago, that the government, which is the source of everything, is made up of gods or demigods, or at least supermen who know the truth and can never err.

Thus communism is not only a total doctrine which is at absolute variance with the deepest persuasions of the West; it is—and this is its importance from the viewpoint of war and peace—a total state. Nor is it just a total state living by itself; it is an aggressive state, absolutely determined to spread its outlook, its system, its power, throughout the world, not indeed under conditions of fair and free competition with other systems and outlooks (this very concept of fair and free competition would of course be the object of vitriolic sarcasm by Marx, Lenin and Stalin), but by force and subversion and every conceivable subtlety.

Communists usually offer one aspect of their teachings to a group or an individual—that aspect which appeals to the interests of the group or the temperament of the individual in question: to the underprivileged masses, it is equality and security and what they call economic justice; to the peoples fighting against colonialism, it is emancipation from their imperialist masters; to soft pacifists, it is attacks against warmongers and petitions for world peace; to oppressed races, it is racial equality; to the cosmopolitans, it is the supranational world scope of communism; to the intellectuals, it is the lure of the ideal of equality and justice; to the liberals, it is what they call the struggle against fascism. Now so far as they go, these partial emphases of communism have each a germ of truth. But they are not the whole truth about communism: they are not the essence of communism. Nor can the abstract good in them stand up, white and radiant, outside the dark shadow of the whole system.

These various aspects of communism are offered as a bait, cunningly prepared to suit the victim, to be followed gradually but steadily by larger and larger doses of the whole system and to be consummated, once the victim is well on his way toward complete capture, by rigid discipline. This seems to be in the general pattern of Communist infiltration: one-sided appeal as a pathway to all-round subjugation. But communism is in reality a compact totality of spirit and values and premises, every one of which essentially partakes of the character of the whole. The greatest danger inherent in communism is not its total evil and falsehood, which is likely, once communism is viewed as a whole, to be rejected even by common sense, but rather the isolated streaks of good and truth which enter into the fabric of the whole and which, viewed in abstraction, may ensnare the weak and innocent.

Superficially, communism is a revolt against the capitalist system, an antithesis to the bourgeois civilization of the 19th and 20th centuries—characterized as it has been by nationalism, individualism, imperialism, politico-economic liberalism, free economic enterprise, private ownership of property and of the means of production, representative government, and the rule of law.

This is of course partly true, although it can be shown that the Soviets are absolutely imperialistic, that in the United Nations they have insisted on nothing more than on the principle of national sovereignty, and that so far as the private ownership of property and of the means of production is concerned, the passage of these things from the private ownership of a few individuals—subject always to the inevitable correctives of free competition and to the social and economic scrutiny of the public and the government—to the monopoly of the state which is subject to no judgment whatsoever above itself, this passage is not a sure mark of progress. Be that as it may, the point I want to make now is that communism has much more in common with its antithesis than it realizes.

Though a revolt against what it ambiguously calls capitalism, communism is more profoundly a completion, a culmination,
a passage to its logical conclusion, of that movement of European secularism and self-estrangement of which the age and
civilization of capitalism is but a product, in fact perhaps an in-
termediate and transitory stage. Their opposition takes place on
common grounds. For behind the opposition between their respective systems of organizing the modes of production and exchange, behind the difference in their patterns of social and
political organization, behind the antithesis of their conceptions
of social dynamics, there lies a basic disturbing kinship of outlook.

It is the kinship of their common underlying *economism*,
their common worship of "the economic man": half-hearted and
perhaps unconscious, yet nevertheless all-pervading, in the one
case, and militant and elevated to the level of a creed, in the
other case. It is the similarity of their common *autonomous humanism*: their preoccupation with human affairs, their concentration on man's life here below, where material interests are
uppermost and material prosperity the supreme good—a concentration which in the one case overshadows and in the other case
entirely supersedes the eternal, the spiritual, the transcendent.
It is finally the similarity of their common *impersonalism*: in
the one case, within the context of an atomistic, self-seeking,
closed and windowless individualism, in itself opaque to love
and suffering and sacrifice and responsibility and social solidarity; and, in the other case, within the context of an absolutely
soulless collectivism in which the person's independent existence
is denied, his freedom, his dignity, his worth being all made
derivative from the leviathan which is his state.

This then is the theory and actuality of communism in general, and this is the character of its dialectic within the secularism of the present Western epoch.

The question therefore arises: Can there be real peace, with
communism so entrenched and so determined? Can the West
get along with this sort of thing? Is the oft-repeated notion of
peaceful coexistence a real possibility?

My answer to all these questions is categorically in the negative. Obviously I cannot get along with one whose whole being not only contradicts mine, but is bent on destroying mine. Therefore when anybody in the West says or has said simply, "We can get along with communism," then one of four propositions is true: (1) either he is a Communist himself; (2) or he is an appeaser; (3) or he does not know what he is talking about; namely, he does not know the nature of the thing with which he says he can get along; (4) or—and this is the most grievous thing—he does not know the supreme values of his own heritage which communism has radically rebelled against and desires to extirpate.

For I assure you it isn't only your soldiers in Korea who are embattled today: it is the highest attainments of mind, spirit, and being of the last four thousand years.

The question therefore is not: Can we get along with communism? Can we arrange a *modus vivendi* between the two worlds? Can we bring about a peaceful coexistence between them? This question, in my opinion, is perfectly stupid. For the West, if it knows itself and if it knows communism, must come to the obvious conclusion that it is absolutely impossible to get along with communism.

What then *is* the question? The question is *whether it is possible to induce, and how to induce, the necessary modification in Communist theory and practice whereby the West then can get along, not indeed with communism as such, but with the Russians.* This is the supreme question of the present generation.

This modification will never take place so long as communism passes from triumph to triumph. Only when communism comes up against hard facts like, for example, Yugoslavia, facts which it cannot alter but which it can fit only by altering itself, will this basic modification emerge. Only then will so-called peaceful coexistence or the policy of live-and-let-live become a possibility.

It is the task of the non-Communist world and especially of the Western world for the sake of peace to create those stubborn and irreducible facts which will force communism *to change itself* and to live at peace with the rest of the world. Four orders of stubborn and irreducible facts must be created. I call them the balance of power, the balance of justice, the balance of mind, and the balance of spirit.

Europe is weak and exposed. The Middle East is weak and exposed. Asia and the Far East are weak and exposed. There is really nothing to prevent communism from walking into these various places from without except the goodness of its heart. Consequently the balance of power at these points must be redressed if there is going to be honest, peaceful coexistence.

Consider, for example, the situation in the Far East. It is not clear whether present Communist China can strike out on an independent path. Entirely apart from ideology, if Communist China must follow the Soviet Union in sheer combination of power, the peaceful balance of the world will be disturbed. These two giants, taken together, will in time constitute a most formidable combination of strength, the like of which the world has never known before. Even if Communists were angels—which I doubt that they are, or at least any more than the rest of us—the rest of the Old World at least will gradually fall into their hands. Therefore, the real problem of war or peace today, so far as the Far East is concerned, is the problem of the independence of China. He works for peace today who works for the independence of China.

Mr. Vishinsky, both last year and this year, in our debates at Lake Success referred to the 600 million or 700 million people who are marching together. Sometimes he used the one figure, sometimes the other. Whichever he uses, the rest of the world is frightened—and not without justification. If 600 or 700 million people are marching together in Mr. Vishinsky's sense, then the necessary peaceful equilibrium of the world is upset, and we are already at war.

The problem of the rest of the world, including the Soviet Union, is to do everything possible to induce the independence of China. Only an independent and free China can restore the balance of power to the Orient, and help restore the balance of power to the rest of the world.

Never has a situation required more experimental openness of mind than the present situation. The real effective and enduring detachment of China, militarily and politically, is the ultimate objective which must always be kept in mind. Whatever can be honorably done to bring about that worthy consummation must be attempted.

What is true of the Far East is also true of Europe. The power vacuum now in Europe must be filled. And I am speaking not only of sheer military power. Beside the power vacuum and perhaps as an underlying cause of it gapes a most disturbing psychological vacuum. The Europeans are not sure of themselves. The communistic-materialistic softening process has been going on in Europe for decades now. The result has been that there is a blurring of values in the European mind. But unless not only the sheer military balance in Europe is redressed, but also the European spirit develops an absolute faith in its values and a determined will to fight for them, I see no possibility of real peace—as a structure of finely equilibrated forces, both physical and moral—in the immediate future.

There are appalling conditions of privation and poverty throughout Asia and many other portions of the world. So long as Moscow means, truly or falsely, hope for the masses, and the Western world does not mean so with the same clarity, it is idle to speak of peaceful coexistence or of live-and-let-live. There is in this regard an unequal appeal to the suffering masses of mankind as between, for example, Moscow and Washington. Communism will then sprout from within, or at least the internal situation will be so softened as to prepare the ground for the easy march of communism from without.

The British Commonwealth of Nations has endeavored in the recent Colombo conference boldly to meet this situation. President Truman's Point Four is a response to the same need. I might remark in this connection that, in my opinion, the present magnitude of operations of the Point Four program must be multiplied by about one hundred times before it can begin to be adequate for the crying needs of the moment. For what are $5 billion devoted to the restoration of the balance of justice between the meaning of Moscow and the meaning of Washington in the mind of the eternally dispossessed of the world?

The balance of mind requires that there be some equality in the accessibility to truth and information between the countries of the iron curtain and the rest of the world. When you sit on United Nations bodies day after day and hear the honorable Communist representatives adduce facts and refer to conditions in the non-Communist world while the rest of us cannot as readily refer to facts and conditions in Communist countries, just because this side of the iron curtain is far more open to Communist inspection than that side to us, you feel deeply perturbed. It is not just that they know about and can criticize conditions outside their realm, while we are physically debarred from knowing except in general and vague terms about conditions in Communist countries. There can be no peace until this injustice is redressed, until there is equal intellectual and social intercourse between the Communist and the non-Communist worlds, until we, on this side of the chasm, have as much access to what goes on beyond as they have to what goes on here. The possibility of real intellectual modification on the part of communism will then become real.

The balance of spirit is in a sense the most important task. For a man, no matter how weak or poor or ignorant, will be exceedingly strong and rich and wise if only he has an idea for which he can die and therefore for which he can live. Communism provides such an idea. The Communists have a purpose in life beyond their immediate cares and worries.

The non-Communist world does not have such a sense of mission. There is, therefore, so far an unequal spiritual struggle between it and the Communist world. So long as this is the case, peaceful coexistence must remain a pious hope. For there will always be an uneasy tension in the minds of men afflicted with the widespread malady of purposelessness. They will always feel they are unjustly cheated of something: the unifying and liberating sense of purpose.

The source of this agonizing injustice is that the Western world, as it seems to me, does not believe strongly enough in the importance and power of ideas. It trusts far more in gadgets and in the manipulation of the emotions than in the truth and potency of ideas. In many instances, Western man is too much

wrapped up in himself, in his own self-pity, his own self-worry
and petty, little problems. He does not sufficiently rest in joy on
the marvelous vision of objective and independent truth, throb-
bing with life and meaning and salvation.

The ideal of taking a college degree, getting married and
settled, rearing a family, having a dependable job, making lots
of money and having a solid and ever expanding bank account
—this ideal conceived purely in these terms is not good enough.
It is, if I may say so, a very timid ideal. It is not dangerous
enough; it does not answer to man's deepest hunger for truth
and community, where going out of one's self is a joy, and
where it is more blessed to give than to receive.

Confronted with this ideal alone, Asia—if I must be frank
with you—is not impressed. In fact, despite all her darkness
and misery, Asia can still do better. And an Asian who knows
something of the highest values which have characterized the
Western positive tradition at its best can turn to the West and
say, "You can do much better also."

If the thirsty souls of honest seeking men throughout the
world are going to be satisfied, a mighty living true faith must
be discovered or created to balance the militant faith of communism. Pure nationalism will always be handicapped by reason
of its particularism, whereas the need in this physically unified
world is for something just as universal as communism but in-
finitely more profound and true. He does not know the infinite
positive hidden riches of the non-Communist world in Asia, in
Europe and in America, who does not believe that such a faith
can be released in it.

The present crisis is therefore a great opportunity. It will
call forth deep searchings of heart which must lead to the find-
ing of adequate spiritual answers. For too long have we buried
and shelved our ultimate values, for too long have we been dis-
tracted from them by lesser things. The day of reckoning has
come when we can no longer afford the luxury of living in the
plains but must rise to the heights where once again the gods
can speak to men.

The tribulation of the days to come will bring upon men
a fresh visitation of destiny, the purification of heart which

comes from contact with the ultimate and awful. And in East
and West alike our spiritual and intellectual leaders will seek
new dimensions and they will find them. They will ask, Is it
true that Marxism is the final dispensation that has canceled and
absorbed all that we have known for thousands of years to be
true and good and noble and ultimate? And they will bless the
names of Marx and Lenin, not indeed for what they did and
meant, but for having roused the rest of us from our slumber
and forced us to inquire after our good and return to our God.

TRUTH AND FREEDOM [8]

HARVEY K. McARTHUR [9]

Dr. Harvey K. McArthur gave this Baccalaureate sermon in the memorial Chapel, at Wellesley College, on Sunday morning, June 11, 1950, at eleven o'clock, before alumnae, 385 members of the class of 1950, and their families. The service was part of the seventy-second annual Commencement. Graduation exercises were held on the following morning.

McArthur's sermon, philosophical and academic, had several homiletic characteristics: the thesis was based upon a Biblical text; the main and sub-propositions were clearly expounded and ordered in logical sequence; the illustrations were largely historical and philosophical, with literary references and with allusions to events of the hour to give practical and definite application to the theme; the insight was thought-provoking; the language, although somewhat theological, was unhackneyed and well adapted to the undergraduate listeners.

Dr. McArthur, following his manuscript, nevertheless communicated easily and effectively. The speaker's pleasant informality was no doubt explained partly by his experience as teacher at Wellesley.

Ye shall know the truth and the truth shall make you free.— John 8:31

These words have become part of our general heritage. They are impressively inscribed on numerous libraries and institutions of learning. They may even adorn some archway here on the Wellesley campus. Unfortunately truths lose their meaning— and sometimes their truth—when they become conventional slogans. What is the real significance of these words which the Gospel of John attributes to Jesus: "Ye shall know the truth and the truth shall make you free"?

There are two significant variables in this sentence: "truth" and "free." These two variables are related to each other, that is to say, the truth we possess determines the nature of our free-

[8] Text and permission for this printing furnished through the courtesy of Dr. McArthur.

[9] For biographical note, see Appendix.

dom; the type of freedom we desire should determine the truth we seek.

The modern world has been characterized by the tremendous growth of a specific type of truth, namely, technical and scientific knowledge. This truth produces its own type of freedom: freedom from nature—freedom from helplessness in the face of nature's normal operations. While this freedom is limited it is a genuine freedom. Clearly John's Gospel was not concerned with this. Nevertheless, it is necessary for us as moderns to evaluate this type of truth and the freedom it brings.

Certain significant technical discoveries were made at the very dawn of human history: the principle of the lever and of the wheel, the use and control of fire, the cultivation of crops, the use of sails. These discoveries increased man's freedom from, and control over, the forces of nature. All subsequent developments would have been impossible except for such basic discoveries. But despite the significance of these initial discoveries it is clear that all of them combined up to the 18th century did not change man's mode of living as much as the discoveries of the most recent two centuries. No romanticizing of the Middle Ages or of the Classical World should blind our eyes to the freedom we have acquired from the discomforts and catastrophes of nature—a freedom for which our ancestors dared not even dream. A few years ago I went to the hospital with a ruptured appendix. Modern science saved my life. Doubtless many others are here today because of similar experiences. To our acquaintances these may not be wholly unambiguous proofs of the blessings of science—but we at least are grateful, and in a thousand ways we have benefited from this type of truth. Unmistakably scientific knowledge and technical know-how have given us increased freedom from the caprice of nature.

And yet, while all this is true, our freedom based upon the control of nature has its drawbacks. Since 1945 no serious discourse is complete without at least one reference to those scientific monstrosities the A-Bomb, and the possible H-Bomb. Let me pay my respects to them now. It is astonishing to hear naïve souls argue seriously that our present predicament is due to a time lag between man's technical and spiritual development. Do they really believe that all would be well if a moritorium were declared on technical discoveries during the next thirty years? Or the next century? Would we then know how to solve the problems arising from the fact that two angry Goliaths glare at each other across a prostrate world. Surely this is an illusion— an evasion of the problem. Technical development surged ahead of spiritual development when the first caveman discovered he could discipline his wife more effectively with a club than with his fist. It has stayed ahead ever since. And if the 20th century goes back to the club stage—as it well may—technical development will still be ahead of spiritual development. It will be ahead for the obvious reason that technical knowledge is cumulative, and it can be transmitted as easily by spiritual morons as by saints. Sometimes more easily! It may be discouraging for those who are just completing four rather stiff academic years— but there is no necessary correlation between knowledge and moral-spiritual development. Increasing power over nature means increasing freedom from nature. But it also means increasing power to destroy. Freedom from nature enslaves us to the machine that freed us, and places us at the mercy of the man who controls that machine.

But apart from the destructive potentialities within scientific knowledge there is the additional unfortunate fact that during the past century this sphere of truth so absorbed our energies that we lost sight of the eternal problems of the human quest. We were so fascinated by what this type of truth could accomplish that we forgot what it could not accomplish. There is no God but science and its realities are the only realities! If our lives can be made longer and more comfortable—what else do we need? Is it significant that in the last *Encyclopedia Britannica* the article on electricity is a hundred pages long, while another hundred pages deal with related subjects; but Epictetus must be satisfied with a single column on a single page? Is it significant that the article on chemistry is fifty-five pages long while the one on Christianity is under eight pages? Perhaps the wealth of new knowledge makes this ratio inevitable, but it suggests a culture concerned with the techniques of living rather than with the meaning or purposes of life.

Francis Thompson, in his poem on the nineteenth century, speaks of science as "the blind worm." "And all the peoples in their turns before the blind worm bowed them down." (This is a line which you are not apt to find in the conventional anthologies of quotations.) More recently T. S. Eliot, addressing the "decent, godless people" of the twentieth century, says,

> Binding the earth and the water to your service,
> Exploiting the seas and developing the mountains,
> Dividing the stars into common and preferred,
> Engaged in devising the perfect refrigerator,
> Engaged in working out a rational morality,
> Engaged in printing as many books as possible,
> Plotting of happiness and flinging empty bottles,
> Turning from your vacancy to fevered enthusiasm
> For nation or race or what you call humanity;
> Though you forget the way to the temple,
> There is one who remembers the way to your door:
> Life you may evade, but death you shall not.
> You shall not deny the stranger.

Or—putting poetry aside and borrowing the irreverent title of a recent book "Science Is a Sacred Cow." (I am confident that the members of the science departments are too intelligent to misunderstand what I am saying!)

In the opening centuries of the Christian era a very different type of truth and freedom was actually propagated by the Stoics. Greek thought had been concerned with freedom, but with the Stoics the question of the individual's interior, spiritual freedom replaced the problem of political freedom—the freedom of the citizen and the city-state. In men such as Seneca, Epictetus, or Marcus Aurelius freedom was the goal of life. They asserted that it was available to all who understood two basic principles or truths. First, everything external, everything outside of moral choice is unimportant, indifferent, adiaphora. Secondly, moral choice is entirely within my own power, and if I recognize the good and the true, I will inevitably follow them.

There is profound insight in the first of these principles, and its acceptance brings a real freedom. My neighbors have a five year old boy. When he tries to go into his house he turns the doorknob. If it does not respond immediately he shouts for his mother. If she does not respond immediately he shakes the door, kicks it, and screams with uninhibited fury. The present speaker finds such conduct very aggravating, and suspects that a dose of Epictetus would be beneficial—though I can conceive of a less subtle approach to the problem that might be equally efficacious. Only—only when I look into the mirror, or when I observe other more or less adult individuals I realize that we all need a dose of Epictetus. We are too concerned with what happens to us. We all need to take more casually the petty annoyances, vicissitudes, and injustices of life. We need this Stoic freedom from fuss!

But though this is true, is it not a distortion, resulting from the Greek body-spirit dualism, to assert that everything—everything!—outside of my own moral choice should be indifferent to me? Should it be a matter of indifference if a loved one dies, or a marriage is broken, or a career disrupted? Or take the world outside the area of self-interest. Should I view the man-made injustices of history with Stoic calm—with apathy? If six million people die in concentration camps, is it enough for me to say that Hitler was clearly not behaving like a true philosopher? Or that if the six million had understood that only moral choice is important they would have been indifferent to their fate?

Relegating the entire realm of historical event to the category of the indifferent may give freedom, but according to the Biblical view it is an illegitimate freedom—a freedom from responsibility. You cannot view the world with apathy and fulfill the injunction "Thou shalt love thy neighbor as thyself," though the Stoics sometimes made the attempt. Marcus Aurelius was undoubtedly a far better emperor than Christian tradition might suggest, but according to Stoic theory he was a good emperor not so much for the sake of his people as in order to preserve the integrity of his own moral choice to fulfill his duty as a member of the unusual city. Fortunately Marcus Aurelius was better than the theory. Unfortunately the church has frequently been worse.

Whenever the church has thought of men simply as souls to be saved, whenever she has ignored the physical aspects of human existence, whenever she has ignored the prophetic tradition, she has failed. And she has failed frequently. It is not surprising that the church is now challenged by a movement which thinks of men simply as bodies to be fed. However, this morning, I am not primarily concerned with the church's responsibility to transform the world. (Was it Peter Marshall who said, "You cannot do much *for* the world until you have done something *with* yourself"?) Over against the Stoics the church has a duty both to transcend *and* to transform the world. To perform the latter task she must view the external world not with the Stoic freedom of apathy but with the Christian commitment of *agapa*, i.e. love.

Furthermore what about the second Stoic affirmation: that we are free if we confine our concern to our own moral choices? The Stoics viewed man's soul as a citadel or fortress. If we withdraw our concern from the external world over which we have little control, if we retreat into the citadel of the soul, all will be harmonious. We will be masters of our destiny. We will be truly free. This is highly plausible. But what if, perchance, "your sickness is your soul"? What if the complexity of the problem of freedom is revealed only when we are alone with ourselves? What if the world is not a snare but an escape from the problem of self? What if the cleft within us, the abyss, the meaninglessness which threatens to overwhelm us—what if these have no solution, until, after withdrawing into ourselves, we again reach outside of ourselves to Him who is neither the world nor ourselves? What if final freedom is discovered not in self, but only after the self has been surrendered with an unconditional surrender to Him who is eternal?

Occasionally the Stoics came close to realizing that the autonomy, the autarchy, of the soul was not as great as they claimed. Epictetus laments that his conduct does not conform to his beliefs. He rephrases an epigram to describe himself and his followers, "Lions in the schoolroom, outside foxes." (If you use that proverb I trust you will apply it to yourselves and not the faculty.) Epictetus cries out in despair, "Show me a true Stoic if you can." Just one—just one. And in a magnificent passage he exclaims, "Great is the struggle, divine the task: the prize is a kingdom, freedom, serenity, peace. Remember God: call upon him to help you and stand by your side." And yet—

just as their dualism prevented the Stoics from understanding the significance of historical events, so their deification of man's spirit or mind prevented a real surrender to Him who is eternal. To call upon God meant—ultimately—to call upon your own best self. There are limits to what can be accomplished by such techniques.

Stoic confidence in the sovereignty of the individual self is distantly paralleled by a tendency common to many of the intelligentsia. (I use the term loosely, very loosely, probably it cannot be used any other way.) Like the Stoics they recognize as illusion much that dominates the life of ordinary mortals. They scorn these illusions—declare themselves emancipated—live out of their individual inspiration and autonomy. Yet their lives have a disconcerting tendency to disintegrate because they have no allegiance, no anchor, outside themselves. It is tragic—and terrifying—to observe a young person who has ability—intelligence—fine training; who analyzes acutely the foibles of popular thought, who believes in all the right causes (that is to say those causes in which I also believe) and yet that person fails to make any constructive contribution to society. His personal life is a failure. I wonder whether the intensity with which some throw themselves into efforts for world reform is compensation—a frantic struggle to create meaning outside lest they be engulfed by the meaninglessness within, by the chaos of their own lives? Could their scorn for the "uninitiated" be envy on the defensive? They find freedom. But their freedom is their undoing!

Biblical faith never assumes that absolute freedom is the prerogative of human beings, or that it is to be formed within the individual self. The freedom which it offers is—paradoxically —a freedom for those who are the servants of God, for those who have abandoned themselves. It is a freedom for the irrevocably committed. In the Synoptics Jesus says, "Whoever would save his life will lose it; and whoever loses his life for my sake and the Gospel's will save it." Paul says, "I have been crucified with Christ—it is no longer I who live but Christ who lives in me." John's Gospel says, "Ye must be born again."

The metaphors differ but all agree that only beyond this spiritual death and resurrection is there true freedom.

Obviously the truth leading to such freedom is a distinctive kind of truth. It is not one abstract proposition in addition to other abstract propositions with which we are already familiar. It is not a discovery, a piece of information, to be fitted into the previously established pattern of our thought—though theological or philosophical speculation is frequently of this character. The liberating truth to which the New Testament writers witness is not information about deity, it is an encounter with the living God. It is the I-Thou relationship Martin Buber describes so effectively. God is not an inanimate object—the helpless prey of our inquisitive minds. He is the Eternal Subject! As Paul would say: It is not simply that we know Him but that we are known by Him.

For those who stand within the main stream of Christian tradition this encounter with the living God is mediated through an encounter with history. And (this is the offense) an encounter with a particular bit of history—an encounter with Jesus of Nazereth. The controversies over the theological definition of the person of Jesus arose from the difficulty of affirming, on the one hand, that he was a genuine segment of genuine history, and, on the other hand, the church's experience that the encounter with him was an encounter with the living God. In modern parlance—the question of the historical and the suprahistorical.

The ethical character of the historical Jesus determines the content of the ethical demand made upon us by the encounter with the living God. For such an encounter makes demands. It is no casual tea-party or cocktail-hour meeting. It is a fateful encounter—an encounter that makes demands. This is the paradox mentioned earlier. God demands that he may give—he wounds that he may heal—he enslaves that he may set free. It is only when we have been drawn out of ourselves that we can be free from ourselves. Men and women in any walk of life may have this freedom by paying the price. The measure of our surrender is the measure of our freedom.

"Ye shall know the truth and the truth shall make you free."

Now I have finished what I had to say. I may not have made myself clear though I have done my best. You are under no obligation to agree with me. But you are under an obligation to face the question of your own inner freedom. So far as most of you are concerned the task of "Educating Our Daughters" is completed—that is, in the formal sense. As graduates of this institution you have undoubtedly acquired knowledge. You may even have acquired a measure of wisdom! But have you—either in school or out of school—found an inner freedom that will sustain you? A freedom that neither totalitarian states nor Atlantic Charters can either give or take away?

COMFORT YE MY PEOPLE [10]

RALPH W. SOCKMAN [11]

Dr. Ralph W. Sockman gave this sermon on Sunday, December 17, 1950, from 10:00 to 10:30 A.M. over the National Broadcasting Company network. It was one of the regular series of the National Radio Pulpit.

Dr. Sockman, since 1917 Pastor of the Madison Avenue Methodist Church (now Christ Church), New York, has grown steadily in leadership and prominence as one of America's outstanding pulpit orators. For more than twenty years he has been active as a radio speaker, and since 1937 has been a preacher with the National Radio Pulpit. The network includes from Sunday to Sunday about sixty stations. Sockman's ministry has been extended also through short wave to other countries.

The following short sermon is typical of his radio sermonic style. (1) He usually uses a text. (2) He usually illustrates his sermons with a biblical narrative (e.g. Isaiah and Jeremiah). (3) He enriches his sermons with biblical references and quotations ("Comfort ye, comfort ye, my people"). (4) He is usually personal ("I have never celebrated Christmas in a very warm clime"), evangelical, and inspirational. (5) His sermons are well constructed. Young clergymen will do well to study the structure for clearness, coherence, relevancy, and proportion of treatment. (6) His illustrations, other than biblical, are numerous and timely (the girl and doll, Park Avenue penthouses, St. Petersburg, Buenos Aires, Korean War). (7) He cites extensively literature and philosophy (Handel, Arab proverb, Edna Ferber, Valley Forge, Lincoln, Whittier, W. A. Quayle, Arthur Clutton Block, C. S. Lewis, Newman). His language is oral, concrete, personal, sometimes vivid. (8) He is careful in articulation, emphatic in tone and gesture, "with plenty of vocal resonance, variety in pitch range and intensity, and with persuasiveness in tone and manner." [12]

During the Advent season each year, the hearts of Christendom are lifted by Handel's "Messiah." It is probably being sung in all our communities. This great oratorio was composed in a

---

[10] Permission for this reprint furnished through the courtesy of the National Broadcasting Company and of Dr. Ralph W. Sockman. Text furnished by the National Radio Pulpit.

[11] For biographical note, see Appendix.

[12] For additional comment on Sockman as a speaker and for examples of his preaching, see *Representative American Speeches: 1942-1943*, p267-75; *Representative American Speeches: 1946-1947*, p271-8; *Representative American Speeches: 1948-1949*, p216-28.

dark time. Handel was living in Ireland during 1741 when Irish people were filled with fears and unrest. And early in 1743, when it was first rendered in London, the English people appeared to be ready for revolution. Morale was low, morals were lax, society seemed decadent. In such a time the opening words of the oratorio would have instant appeal. Hear them: "Comfort ye, comfort ye my people, saith your God."

These words, as you know, came out of Israel's dark days. They are the opening sentence of the fortieth chapter of Isaiah, one of the most magnificently moving passages in all literature. The prophet felt called of God to comfort his people after their defeats and afflictions. Comfort, let us remember, as used in the Bible is a word which means to strengthen rather than to soothe, to put courage and nerve into men's hearts rather than to lull them to rest.

And now we are approaching Christmas 1950 and we are in America, the strongest nation of the world, which has just suffered one of the severest setbacks in all its history. Our leadership is challenged. Our armies have been in retreat. And although this is not absolutely a new experience, it is a rare one. If ever we needed the strength-building comfort of God, that time is now. Let us then in our dark time ponder these words which broke from the lips of the prophet in the dark hours of his nation and burst into music through Handel's "Messiah" in the dark period of Britain. "Comfort ye, comfort ye my people, saith your God."

And what are the grounds of comfort which the prophet has to offer? The first is that he reminds his countrymen of the *troubles they have survived*. Every mature person can take heart from the fact that he has faced dark times before and has come through. Herein is a difference between maturity and childishness.

The little girl breaks her doll, and her heart is broken. Her mother may remind her that she broke a doll a week before and Daddy brought her a new one. But that does not comfort the little girl. Her mother may promise her a new toy next week. But the little thing cannot comprehend next week. The tiny child is a frail bark on a sea uncharted by her and every storm of sorrow is an engulfing cloud through which she cannot see.

But as we grow to maturity we normally gain perspective. We discover that the sea of life has storms which turn its smoothness rough. Yet the waves which roll have both trough and crest. And from the trough we can rise toward the crest if we keep the mastery of our craft. Hence the mature person, as Saint Paul says, comes through the period when he thought as a child and spoke as a child and finds at least three things that abide—faith, hope and love.

And not only do faith, hope and love survive the heartbreaks but they come through enriched and strengthened by the storms they have survived. In fact we would develop no such thing as faith if all were clear sailing, for faith is the conviction of things we have not seen. And there would be no such quality as hope if there were no darkness, for hope gets its growth in dark places. And there would be no love worthy the name, if there were no uncertainty and sacrifice to call it forth. As the old Arab proverb puts it, "All sunshine makes a desert."

Thus we can draw comfort not only from the fact that we have survived past troubles but also that in doing so life has gained new dimensions and meaning. Look around us. Do we not know persons who have been so uniformly successful that their souls have grown small and hard? And do we not know persons who have so steadily sought the easy safe paths that their souls have become small and soft? These latter are like the character Edna Ferber pictured in her book, "So Big." The heroine of that book was a pioneer woman who came through the hardships and struggles of the Midwest strong and resourceful. But her son, basking in the sunshine of his mother's success, had always sought the easy paths. At last, his mother saw him for what he was, smug, weak, soft, and she exclaimed sadly, "You're just too smooth."

In contrast, look at the person who has weathered the storms of trouble. Those lines etched in his face by suffering, how they give character to his countenance! What if Jesus had lived a life of unbroken worldly success? What if his popularity as a teacher in Galilee had gone on growing and he had ended his career as the most popular preacher in Palestine's history with no heckling critics, no crown of thorns, no cross? Of such a One we should not sing today: "Jesus Lover of my Soul, let me to thy bosom fly." Without the scars Jesus would never have become our comforter. Without the cross he would not be our Savior.

Now, this fact that troubles survived give dimension and dignity to life should be a source of comfort to us in our present national darkness. We came through worse times than the present when our soldiers were freezing, not in faraway Korea, but in near-by Valley Forge. Without the reverses and retreats which Washington went through, he would not be the Washington we revere today. If Washington had been unbrokenly successful, he might have been "first in war"; he might even have been "first in peace"; but he would not be "first in the hearts of his countrymen." America went through darker times than now in 1861 to 1865. And the lines in the face of Lincoln and the grey in the hair of Lee served to make them beloved of posterity.

We faced darker days than these just nine years ago this month after Pearl Harbor. And we came through to a unity never known before. Do not misunderstand me. I am not implying that God sends wars to develop men's souls. God does not send wars. They come through man's sin. But when men drift into war through stupidity and devilishness, they somehow in the darkness discover new dimensions in life, which, if discovered in peacetime would have prevented war.

Great living is not a lilting melody played in the middle register. It is a symphony with deep undertones of tragedy. We are hearing these deep notes now. But let us take heart from the troubles we have survived and the greatness that comes through suffering.

A second ground of comfort suggested by Isaiah is the *divine love revealed as enduring through all reverses*. Note the pronouns in the words, "Comfort ye, comfort ye my people" saith *your* God." God calls you "my" people, and he is "your" God.

When do we come to feel God's love most vividly, in our sufferings or in our successes? Well, let us take it on the human level first. When does our human love become most convincing and comforting, in the sharing of prosperity or of suffering? The divorce records give the answer to that question. Homes break much more frequently in Park Avenue penthouses than on the farms.

So in our relationship with God, we feel His vital presence in times of hardship more than in hours of ease. For instance, note the perfunctory and indifferent attitude of a sleek comfortable crowd as some minister returns thanks before a big public dinner. Contrast that with the serious but receptive attention of mourners at a grave when the preacher prays, "We give thee thanks for the good examples of all those thy servants who have departed this life in peace." Yes, it is very noticeable that those who are most confident of God's goodness are those who might seem to have least reason for being so.

Whittier once wrote a poem "The Eternal Goodness." When did he write it? When all was going well? Not at all. He wrote it in the year 1865 when dark days of war were merging into the darkness of a so-called Reconstruction Era. Listen to Whittier's words:

> I see the wrong that round me lies,
>   I feel the guilt within,
> I hear, with groans and travail cries,
>   The world confess its sin.
>
> Yet in the maddening maze of things,
>   And tossed by storm and flood
> To one fixed trust my spirit clings,
>   I know that God is good.

We are now approaching Christmas. We need ever to remember that the Nativity came to a people prepared by long anxious watchfulness. "The people that sat in darkness, upon them hath the light shined." Would Bethlehem have its full rich meaning without the dark background?

I have never celebrated Christmas in a very warm clime. Many of my friends go to Florida and they tell me Saint Petersburg and Miami are ideal places for Christmas. And my friends in Los Angeles tell me that southern California is a perfect place to spend Christmas or Easter or eternity! But this summer in

Buenos Aires, I met a friend who frankly told me that down there where December is summer it is hard to get the feel of Christmas on a bathing beach. Perhaps it is only tradition which has come to make us associate Christmas with snow and warm fires and cozy rooms. Nevertheless, the warm lighted rooms sheltered from the wintry wind are symbolically suggestive of the Bethlehem spirit. The manger scene was against the dark backdrop of a cold inn-keeper, a cruel Herod. Christ came as the light of the world, and it is in the darkness and cold that we appreciate light most.

And the Bible pictures God as a Father who not only comes to us in our darkness but watches over us. The late Bishop William A. Quayle, one of the beloved mystics of the Methodist Church, once told of wrestling with a personal problem through a long wakeful night. He was pacing the floor about two o'clock in the morning, when he seemed to hear God say to him: "Quayle, you go to bed. I'll sit up the rest of the night." To some of you, that may seem too simple a way to get peace of mind, but it worked in that case.

In our funeral service one of the most favored scripture readings is the 121st Psalm. In it are these words: "He will not suffer thy foot to be moved: he that keepeth thee will not slumber." The other day I read those words to a sorrowing family. The day was so stormy that the cold winds drove us back rather quickly from the exposed hillside grave to the warmth of our homes. But the comforting thought came to me that a God who slumbereth not would silently keep watch over that grave during the blustering night. Oh, I know that the spirit of the departed was not in that mound of earth, but nevertheless, the psalmist's words made me aware of God's watchful care.

And in the present difficulties of our national situations, I am comforted by the thought of God coming to us in darkness and watching over us in darkness. I think Americans are doing more praying to God right now than in times of prosperity. And I believe our people will heed the national call to prayer two weeks from today. While our progress may not stop the Chinese Communists at Korea's thirty-eighth parallel, I am confident that a praying America will eventually find a way to check communism.

Last June through the United Nations we took our stand on the principle that international police force must replace the war system as waged by nations taking law into their own hands. If we stand firmly for that principle, keep our motives pure and our methods above reproach by the sincerely peace-loving nations, we shall not be defeated. Though right may now seem to be "on the scaffold" and wrong may seem to be "on the throne," yet God standeth "within the shadow keeping watch above his own." And if we try as best we know to be on God's side with righteousness and justice, time is on our side too.

When the prophet Isaiah heard God's command, "Comfort ye, comfort ye my people," he found still a third ground for comfort. The people would take heart not only from the troubles survived and the divine love revealed as enduring, but also from the *divine power still creative*.

May I ask you a question? How do you think the historian of the year 2,000 A.D. will characterize this decade at the middle of the twentieth century? I suppose for some time we shall remember 1950 as the year of the Korean War. And ever since the atom bomb was dropped in 1945, we have been terming this the Atomic Age. But my prediction is that the historian of fifty years hence will call this the *World Organization Age*. The event which takes precedence over every other event because of its importance to every other event of our time is the shaping of a world community. The greatest thing about our time is not that it is the atomizing age but the organizing age.

Of course, in bringing to birth a world community, there are the pains of travail. So severe are those pains at the present moment that some think we are in at a death rather than a birth. But my faith is akin to that of Jeremiah the prophet. He had a two-fold vision. He saw a seething cauldron, symbol of the dangers which threatened his people from a hostile nation. But he saw also the bud of the almond tree. In Palestine the almond tree by its budding gave the first sign of Spring. Thus Jeremiah beheld the stirring of hope under the wintry surface of circumstances.

I would not minimize the dangers of the moment. I would not cry "peace, peace" when there is no peace. But when we look over the world, we see the millions waking to the possibilities of a better life; we see them yearning for the day when each can sit under his own vine and fig tree and not be afraid; we see the common people growingly aware that peace is not possible without world organization; we hear the parents of the various nations calling for leaders who have such a will to peace that they will find a way to peace. These are some of the signs which make me feel that this will be remembered as the World Organizing Age rather than as the Atomic Age.

I do not often quote from the *Reader's Digest* because its contents are familiar to so many of you. But in the current number is a story which not only moves me but strikes me as a miniature which might be enlarged for our nation at this hour. It is the story of a man who was in charge of the "dead letter" department in an English post office. He lost a little son. His loss made him so bitter that he would lie at night staring with open eyes and hardened face. He shut himself into himself, away from his wife and little daughter.

Just before Christmas a "dead letter" came across his desk, addressed to "Santa Claus, North Pole." He was about to toss it into the waste basket, but he opened it. This is part of what he read:

Dear Santa: We are very sad at our house this year and I don't want you to bring me anything. My little brother went to Heaven last spring. All I want you to do when you come to our house is to take brother's toys to him. I'll leave them in the corner by the kitchen stove. . . . I know he'll be lost up in Heaven without them, most of all his horse; he always liked riding it so much. . . . If you could give Daddy something that would make him like he used to be, and tell me stories, I do wish you would. . . . And I will be your good little girl.

When the grief-stricken father finished reading, he braced his shoulders and went back to his wife and little daughter and he was smiling just as he used to do. To suffer our losses and then to serve what is left, with gallant courage, discovering that

God gives us strength equal to our days, and using our sorrows to make the finer stuff of character—that is great living.

Lift the story to the scale of our nation, and what does it suggest? That even out of times like these, America, still the strongest nation in the world, can make her bigness into greatness.

Handel began his oratorio "The Messiah" with the words, "Comfort ye, comfort ye my people." But the music and theme rise to such a triumphant crescendo that when it reaches the closing Hallelujah Chorus, audiences ever since its opening presentation over two hundred years ago have stood to their feet. That, my friends, is a fitting symbol of our Christian faith.

APPENDIX

.

BIOGRAPHICAL NOTES [1]

ACHESON, DEAN GOODERHAM (1893-   ). Born in Middleton, Connecticut; B.A., Yale, 1915; LL.B., Harvard, 1918; honorary M.A., Yale, 1936; LL.D., Wesleyan, 1947; private secretary to Louis D. Brandeis, 1919-21; practiced law, 1921-33; Under-Secretary of Treasury (resigned 1933); practiced law, 1934-41; Assistant Secretary of State, 1946-47; Under Secretary of State, 1947; practiced law, 1947-48; Secretary of State since January 1949; Ensign, U. S. Navy, World War I; member, Delta Kappa Epsilon, Scroll and Key. (See also *Current Biography: 1949.*)

AUSTIN, WARREN ROBINSON (1877-   ). Born in Highgate, Vermont; Ph.B., University of Vermont, 1899; LL.D., Vermont, 1932, Columbia University, 1944, Norwich University, 1944; studied law, St. Albans, Vermont, 1899-1902; admitted to Vermont bar, 1902; Circuit Court of United States, 1906; Supreme Court of United States, 1914; Attorney, American International Corporation in China, 1916-17; elected United States Senator (Republican), 1931, reelected 1934, 1940; President Vermont Bar Association, 1923; studied Palestine conditions, 1936; Puerto Rico judicial system, 1937; American delegate to Chapultepec Conference, 1945; head of the American delegation to the United Nations General Assembly since 1946. (See also *Current Biography: 1944.*)

BARUCH, BERNARD MANNES (1870-   ). A.B., College of the City of New York, 1889; LL.D., Williams, 1923, University of South Carolina, 1925, and several other colleges and uni-

[1] The chief sources of these notes are *Who's Who in America, Current Biography, Religious Leaders in America, International Who's Who, Who's Who in American Education, Directory of American Scholars,* and *The Congressional Directory.*

versities; member of New York Stock Exchange, many years; appointed by President Wilson, member of Advisory Committee on National Defense, 1916; member various committees on war production, World War I; chairman, War Industries Board, 1918; member, Supreme Economic Council; economic adviser for American Peace Commission, 1919; member, President's Conference for Labor and Capital, October 1919; President's Agricultural Conference, 1922; unofficial adviser, various war committees, World War II; American delegate, Atomic Bomb Commission, 1946; awarded many decorations for services in World War I; member, Phi Beta Kappa; author, *Making of Economic and Reparations Sections of Peace Treaty*, 1920, also treatises on various economic subjects. (See also *Current Biography: 1950.*)

DOUGLAS, PAUL HOWARD (1892-   ). Born in Salem, Massachusetts; A.B., Bowdoin, 1913; A.M., Columbia, 1915, Ph.D., 1921; instructor in economics, University of Illinois, 1916-17; Reed College, 1917-18; associate professor of economics, University of Washington, 1919-20; successively, assistant professor, associate professor, and professor of industrial relations, University of Chicago, since 1920; service on many commissions related to unemployment; Guggenheim fellowship, 1931; member Advisory Committee to U. S. Senate and Social Security Board, 1937; private, later major, in Marine Corps, 1942-45; wounded, battle of Okinawa; awarded Bronze Star for heroic service; U. S. Senator from Illinois since 1948; member, Phi Beta Kappa, and other learned societies; author of *Wages and the Family,* 1925; *Theory of Wages,* 1934; and some dozen other books. (See also *Current Biography: 1949.*)

DULLES, JOHN FOSTER (1888-   ). Born in Washington, D.C.; B.A., Princeton, 1908, LL.D., 1946; Sorbonne, Paris, 1908-09; LL.B., George Washington University, 1911; LL.D., Tufts, Wagner, Northwestern; began law practice, New York City, 1911; director, Bank of New York; trustee, Rockefeller Foundation; chairman, Carnegie Endowment for International Peace; chairman, Federal Council of Churches Commission on a Just and Durable Peace; secretary, Hague Peace Conference, 1907; captain and major, U. S. Army, 1917-18; counsel, American Commission to Negotiate Peace, 1918-19; member Reparations Commission and Supreme Economic Council, 1919; member, United States delegation, San Francisco Conference on World Organization, 1945; Council of Foreign Ministers, London, 1945; General Assembly, United Nations, 1946; Meeting of Council of Foreign Ministers, Moscow, 1947; London meeting of "Big Four," 1947; U. S. Senator from New York, July-November 1949 (to complete term of Senator Wagner); appointed counsellor, Department of State, April 1950; appointed, with rank of Ambassador to negotiate terms of peace for Japan, 1951; Phi Beta Kappa; writer and speaker on international affairs. (See also *Current Biography: 1944.*)

EISENHOWER, DWIGHT DAVID (1890-   ). Born in Denison, Texas; B.S., United States Military Academy, 1915; Army Tank School, 1921; graduate, War College, 1929; 2nd Lieutenant, U. S. Army, 1915; Lieutenant Colonel, Tank Corps, World War I; advanced through grades to General of the Army, December 1944; Chief of Operations Division, Office of Chief of Staff, 1942; Commanding General, European Theatre of Operations, June 1942; Allied Commander in Chief, North Africa, November 1942; Supreme Commander of Allied Land, Sea, and Air Forces in Western Europe, November, 1943; Chief of Staff, U. S. Army, 1945-48; elected President of Columbia University, 1948; appointed Supreme Commander of the North Atlantic Treaty Nations, 1950; Author of *Crusade in Europe,* 1948, *Eisenhower Speaks,* 1948. (See also *Current Biography: 1948.*)

HOOVER, HERBERT CLARK (1874-   ). Born in West Branch, Iowa; B.A., in engineering, Stanford, 1895; honorary degrees from Brown University, Columbia, Johns Hopkins, Oxford, Prague, and other institutions here and abroad; United States Food Administrator, 1917-19; director of various relief organizations for the war-stricken nations of Europe; appointed Secretary of Commerce in 1921; President of the United States,

1929-33; coordinator of food supplies to thirty-eight countries, 1946; chairman of Committee on Organization of the Executive Branch of the Government, 1947-49; member Advisory Board, World Bank Reconstruction and Development; author of *American Individualism,* 1922; *The Challenge to Liberty,* 1934; *Addresses upon the American Road,* 1948-50; and numerous addresses on government. (See also *Current Biography: 1943.*)

JOHNSTON, ERIC ALLEN (1896-   ). Born in Washington, D.C., soon moved to Spokane, Washington; LL.B., University of Washington, 1917; captain, marines, 1917-22; entered business 1922 and later was co-owner and president of large electrical contracting and electrical manufacturing companies; president of Spokane Chamber of Commerce, 1931-32; director United States Chamber of Commerce, 1943, vice-president, 1941, president, 1942-46 (four terms); visited South America, Great Britain, and Russia, 1943; president of Motion Picture Association of America 1945-50; member Publicity Advisory Board, Economic Cooperation Administration, 1948; Administrator, Economic Stabilization Agency, since 1950; author of *America Unlimited,* 1944. (See also *Current Biography: 1943.*)

LODGE, HENRY CABOT, JR. (1902-   ). Born in Nahant, Massachusetts; grandson of the late Senator Henry Cabot Lodge; A.B., Harvard, 1924; with Boston *Evening Transcript,* 1923; New York *Herald Tribune,* 1924; member of the Massachusetts General Court, 1933-36; elected to United States Senate from Massachusetts, 1936, for term ending 1943; on leave, major in U. S. Army Tank Corps, with British forces, 1942; Lieutenant Colonel, Southern France, Rhine, and Southern Germany, 1944-45; reelected to U. S. Senate 1946 for term ending January 1953. (See also *Current Biography: 1943.*)

MCARTHUR, HARVEY K. (1912-   ). Born, Billingsville, Missouri; Ph.B., Wheaton College, 1933; Th.B., Westminster Theological Seminary, 1937; Universities of Berlin and Tübingen, 1937-38; S.T.M., Hartford Theological Seminary, 1940; Ph.D., Hartford Seminary Foundation, 1941; University of Glasgow, 1945; Union Theological Seminary, 1946; Instructor, Biblical History, Wellesley College, 1947-48; Associate Professor of New Testament, Hartford Theological Seminary since 1948.

MacLeish, Archibald (1892-   ). Born in Glencoe, Illinois; educated Hotchkiss School; A.B., Yale, 1915, Litt.D., 1939; LL.B., Harvard, 1919; honorary degrees from Tufts, Wesleyan, Colby, Pennsylvania, Johns Hopkins; captain, First World War; author of *The Plot of Earth* (verse), 1925; *Conquistador* (Pulitzer poetry prize), 1932; *Public Speech* (verse), 1936; *The Fall of the City* (verse play for radio), 1937, and other works; Librarian of Congress 1939-44; Director of Office of Facts and Figures, 1941-43; Assistant Secretary of State, 1944-45; Boylston Professor of Rhetoric and Oratory, Harvard University, since 1950. (See also *Current Biography: 1940.*)

Malik, Charles Habib (1906-   ). Born at Bitirram, Al-Koura, Lebanon; educated at the American Tripoli Boys' High School, 1920-23; B.A., American University of Beirut, 1927; M.A., 1934; Ph.D., Harvard, 1937; student, Freiburg University, Germany, 1935-36; assistant in philosophy, Harvard, 1936-37; instructor in philosophy, adjunct professor, and professor and head of the department, successively, at the American University, Beirut, 1937-45; envoy and minister, Republic of Lebanon, to the United States since 1945; delegate of Lebanon to sessions of the General Assembly of the United Nations since 1946; President of the Economic and Social Committee of the United Nations, 1948.

Murray, Philip (1886-   ). Born in Blantyre, Scotland; came to the United States, 1902, naturalized, 1911; member, International Board of United Mine Workers of America, 1912, international vice president, 1920; president of Congress of Industrial Organizations since 1940; member of numerous governmental commissions on labor problems. (See also *Current Biography: 1949.*)

PHILLIPS, HAROLD COOKE (1892-   ). Born in Westmoreland, Jamaica, British West Indies; B.A., Denison University, 1919, L.H.D., 1939; M.A., Columbia, 1922; B.D., Union Theological Seminary, 1922; D.D., Wesleyan, 1929; LL.D., Beloit, 1946; naturalized, 1922; entered Baptist ministry, 1922; pastor, First Church, Mt. Vernon, N.Y., 1922-28; First Church, Cleveland, Ohio, since 1928; Lyman Beecher lecturer at Yale, 1947; author: *Life That Is Life Indeed*, 1928, *Bearing Witness to the Truth*, 1949, and several other volumes of sermons or lectures; member Phi Beta Kappa.

RAHSKOPF, HORACE G. (1897-   ). Born in Olivia, Minnesota; A.B., Willamette University, 1920; Curry School of Expression, 1921; M.A. Iowa, 1927, Ph.D., 1935; assistant professor of speech, University of Washington, 1928; associate professor, 1936, professor, 1943, executive officer of the department, 1947; president of the Washington State Speech Association, 1933-34; associate editor of the *Quarterly Journal of Speech*, 1939-41; president of the Western Speech Association, 1944-45; adviser on speech curriculum, Washington State Office of Public Instruction, 1943-44; president of the Speech Association of America, 1950.

SMITH, MARGARET CHASE (1897-   ). Born at Skowhegan, Maine; student Skowhegan High School, 1912-16; married Clyde Smith, 1930 (died 1940); teacher, Skowhegan, 1916; office executive, Skowhegan *Independent Reporter*, 1919-1928; treasurer, New England Process Company, 1928-30; member of the Republican State Committee, Maine, 1930-36; member of Congress, second Maine District, 1940-49; elected to the United States Senate, 1948. Republican. (See also *Current Biography: 1945.*)

SOCKMAN, RALPH WASHINGTON (1889-   ). Born in Mount Vernon, Ohio. Educated at Ohio Wesleyan University, B.A., 1911, D.D., 1923; Columbia University, M.A., 1913, Ph.D., 1917; Union Theological Seminary, graduate, 1916; numerous honorary degrees; minister, Madison Avenue Methodist Church (now Christ Church) New York City, since 1917; preacher, National Radio Pulpit, since 1937; Lyman Beecher lecturer at Yale, 1941; trustee of a number of colleges and universities; member of Phi Beta Kappa, Delta Sigma Rho; author, *Live for Tomorrow*, 1939; *How to Live*, 1946; and numerous other volumes on religion. (See also *Current Biography: 1946*.)

STERLING, JOHN EWART WALLACE (1906-   ). Born in Linwood, Ontario; B.A., University of Toronto, 1927; M.A., University of Alberta, 1930; Ph.D., Stanford, 1938; lecturer in history, Regina College, 1927-28; assistant instructor in history, University of Alberta, 1920-30; research staff, Hoover War Library, Stanford, 1932-37; instructor in history, 1935-37; assistant professor, 1937-40; associate professor, 1940-42; professor of history 1942, 1949; president of Stanford since October 1949. Fellow, Social Science Research Council, 1939-40; editor (with others) *Features and Figures of the Past*, 1939.

TAFT, ROBERT ALPHONSO (1889-   ). Born in Cincinnati, Ohio; attended public schools of Cincinnati and the Taft School, Watertown, Conn.; A.B., Yale University, 1910; LL.B., Harvard University, 1913; attorney at law; assistant counsel for the United States Food Administration, 1917-18; counsel for the American Relief Administration, 1919; Republican member of the Ohio House of Representatives, 1921-26, speaker, 1926; Ohio State Senate, 1931-32; United States Senate, since 1939; candidate for presidential nomination on Republican ticket, 1948. (See also *Current Biography: 1948*.)

TRUMAN, HARRY S. (1894-   ). Born in Lamar, Missouri; student, Kansas City School of Law, 1923-25; captain, Field Artillery, World War I; judge, Jackson County Court, 1922-24; presiding judge, 1926-34; United States Senator from Missouri, 1935-41, reelected for the term 1941-47; elected Vice President of the United States on the Democratic ticket, November 1944; sworn in as President on the death of President Roosevelt, April 1945; elected President in 1948. (See also *Current Biography: 1945*.)

CUMULATED AUTHOR INDEX

An author index to the volumes of *Representative American Speeches* for the years 1937-1938 through 1950-1951. The date following the title of each speech indicates the volume in which it appears.

SPEECH AND DEBATING

Competitive Debate: Rules and Strategy. By G. M. Musgrave. 151p. rev. ed. 1946. $1.25.

Discussion Methods: Explained and Illustrated. By J. V. Garland. 376p. 3d ed. rev. 1951. $3.

Extempore Speaking: A Handbook for the Student, the Coach, and the Judge. By D. L. Holley. 115p. 1947. $1.50.

High School Forensics: An Integrated Program. By A. E. Melzer. 153p. 1940. 90c.

How to Debate. By H. B. Summers, F. L. Whan, and T. A. Rousse. rev. ed. 349p. 1950. $2.75.

Representative American Speeches. By A. C. Baird, comp. Published annually in The Reference Shelf. Prices vary.

Each volume contains representative speeches by eminent men and women on public occasions during the year. Each speech is prefaced by a short sketch of the speaker and the occasion.

Selected Readings in Rhetoric and Public Speaking. By Lester Thonssen, comp. 324p. 1942. $3.